Path of the
Green Witch

Brittany Nightshade

Nightshade Apothecary Publishing

Table of Contents

Introduction

Ever since I was a child, I've always felt a deep and powerful connection to nature. As a child I would spend countless hours exploring the woods behind my parents' property, picking wildflowers, climbing trees, and making seemingly never-ending trails that meandered through the forest like a faerie's labyrinth. My brothers and I would swim in creeks as cold as ice with water so clear you could see every stone, crustacean and tiny fish that populated its rocky bed. We'd cross through ancient barbed wire fences and make mud pies on the banks of the pond of our neighbor's property, a pastime that would generally devolve into a mud fight, with globs of earth being flung in all directions, after which we'd have to either wash off in the creek or get hosed off back at the house.

My love for nature only grew stronger as I got older. I would spend entire afternoons hiking in nearby forests, listening to the rustling of leaves and the chirping of birds. One of the best things about growing up in Alabama is the vast woodlands at the foothills of the Appalachian mountains, full of moss-covered trails lined with mushrooms and leading to the most beautiful and clean swimming holes and magnificent waterfalls. I felt a sense of peace and belonging in these quiet places and would try to spend as much time as I could exploring these vast areas.

As I entered my adult years my connection to nature began to take on a more spiritual dimension. I began to feel that there was something sacred about the natural world, something that spoke to a deeper part of my being. I would spend hours meditating in the woods and letting the sounds and smells of the forest wash over me and calm my spirit.

It was during this time that I began to develop a particular affinity for wooded groves. There was something magical about these small, secluded spaces, with their dappled sunlight and tangled undergrowth. I would seek them out whenever I could, sometimes spending entire afternoons lying in the grass, watching the leaves dance in the breeze.

My connection to nature wasn't just a solitary one, however. I was fortunate enough to have a few close friends who shared my love for the outdoors. We would spend weekends camping in the woods, telling stories around the campfire and marveling at the stars above us. These experiences only deepened my sense of connection to the natural world, and I felt grateful for every moment spent in its embrace.

As I grow into my mid-thirties, my connection to nature remains a constant presence in my life. Even as I pursue a career and raise a family, I make sure to set aside time for regular hikes and outdoor adventures. I found that these experiences not only continued to nourish my spirit, but also helped me to stay grounded and centered amidst the busyness of daily life.

Looking back, I can see how my love for nature has shaped so much of who I am. It has taught me to slow down and appreciate the small things, to find joy in the simple act of being alive. It has shown me that there is a profound beauty in the world, one that can be found in the quietest of places if we are willing to seek it out. And it has given me a sense of connection to something larger than myself, a feeling of belonging to a world that is vast and mysterious and endlessly wondrous.

Understanding Green Witchcraft

Path of the Green Witch

The term "Green Witch" refers to a particular path within modern witchcraft that emphasizes a deep connection with nature, the natural world, and the use of plants and herbs in practice, using them for medicinal purposes, magical spells, and rituals. The Green Witch Path is a nature-based spiritual path that honors the cycles of the earth and the seasons, and views all of nature as sacred. We also work with other natural elements, such as stones, crystals, and water. We believe in the power of nature to heal and transform, and often incorporate practices such as foraging, herbalism, gardening, and wildcrafting into our daily lives. It is important for us to protect and conserve the natural world, advocate for environmental causes, and engage in sustainable living practices. In addition to our relationship with nature, as green witches we also work with spirits and energies, both within ourselves and in the world around us. We may work with ancestor spirits, animal spirits, or elemental energies, among others. We may also incorporate divination practices, such as tarot or astrology, into our work. We typically have a deep reverence for the cycles of the seasons and the natural world. We may celebrate the solstices, equinoxes, and other seasonal holidays, and may also engage in rituals and practices that honor the cycles of the moon. These practices may include meditation, chanting, or other forms of energy work. The Green Witch Path is a deeply personal one, and each practitioner may interpret and incorporate its practices in their own unique way. Some may focus more on herbalism and plant magic, while others may work more with divination or spirit work. Ultimately, the Green Witch Path is about cultivating a deep connection with nature and using that connection to facilitate healing, transformation, and spiritual growth.

History of Green Witchcraft

Green Witchcraft, a nature-based spiritual tradition, has evolved over time as an amalgamation of various historical and cultural influences. Its roots can be traced back to ancient pagan practices and traditional healing methods from around the world, which focused on the power of plants, herbs, and the elements for healing and spiritual growth. The history of Green Witchcraft is a rich tapestry, weaving together diverse beliefs and practices that have culminated in the contemporary pagan practice we know today. In this chapter, we will explore the key moments and figures in the history of Green Witchcraft and examine the factors that led to the emergence of modern pagan practice.

The seeds of Green Witchcraft can be found in the earliest human civilizations, where people looked to the natural world for answers to their spiritual and physical needs. Ancient cultures revered the Earth, the elements, and the cycles of nature, creating rituals and ceremonies that honored the changing seasons, the fertility of the land, and the interconnectedness of all life. In these early societies, healers and shamans played crucial roles, tapping into the energies of the Earth and using plants and herbs for healing, divination, and spiritual guidance.

In ancient Greece and Rome, the use of herbal medicine and natural healing methods was widespread. Renowned physicians like Hippocrates and Galen advocated for a holistic approach to medicine, emphasizing the importance of diet, exercise, and the use of natural remedies. The Greeks and Romans also held a deep reverence for nature, with gods and goddesses representing various aspects of the Earth, the elements, and the seasons. This reverence for nature and its healing powers is a crucial aspect of Green Witchcraft, and the ancient Greek and Roman beliefs have left a lasting impact on the practice.

Indigenous cultures worldwide have long-held knowledge of the power of plants and herbs for healing and spiritual growth. These ancient healing practices, passed down through generations, often involve a deep connection with the land, the elements, and the spirits of nature. Medicine women and shamans in these cultures possess an intimate understanding of the natural world, using plants, minerals, and other organic substances to treat a wide array of ailments. The wisdom of indigenous cultures has played a significant role in shaping the practice of Green Witchcraft, as modern practitioners continue to learn from and honor these ancient traditions.

In medieval Europe, folk healers and wise women were integral to the health and well-being of their communities.

13

They relied on a deep knowledge of plants and herbs to treat illness and maintain balance within the body and the spirit. However, with the rise of Christianity, these traditional healing practices were increasingly seen as a threat to the established religious order. As a result, the witch trials of the 16th and 17th centuries led to the persecution and execution of thousands of individuals, primarily women, who were accused of practicing witchcraft and using natural remedies for healing.

Despite the persecution and loss of knowledge during the witch trials, the connection to the Earth and the use of natural remedies persisted in various forms. In the early 20th century, a renewed interest in pagan spirituality led to the revival of witchcraft and the development of modern forms of nature-based spiritual practices, such as Wicca. Founded by Gerald Gardner in the 1950s, Wicca drew upon the remnants of European witchcraft traditions, as well as influences from ancient pagan religions, Eastern philosophies, and the emerging environmental movement.

As a distinct tradition within the broader pagan and Wiccan movements, Green Witchcraft emerged in the latter half of the 20th century, characterized by a deep reverence for the natural world and a commitment to environmentalism and sustainability. Pioneers in the field, such as British author and witch Doreen Valiente, played an instrumental role in shaping modern Green Witchcraft. Valiente's book "Natural Magic," published in 1975, emphasized the importance of connecting with the natural world and working with natural materials like herbs and stones in magical and healing practices.

Another influential figure in the history of Green Witchcraft is the American herbalist and author Susun Weed. Weed's work has been crucial in popularizing herbalism and other nature-based healing practices in the United States and beyond, inspiring many modern practitioners of Green Witchcraft. Her writings, along with those of other contemporary authors like Starhawk, Scott Cunningham, and Phyllis Curott, have contributed to the development of a vibrant and diverse Green Witchcraft tradition.

As environmental concerns grew during the late 20th and early 21st centuries, Green Witchcraft adapted and evolved to address the needs of modern practitioners. Many Green Witches now emphasize the importance of sustainability, environmental stewardship, and ecological activism as integral parts of their spiritual practice. This contemporary focus on the Earth's well-being reflects the inherent connection between Green Witchcraft and the natural world, and it serves as a reminder of the responsibility that Green Witches have to protect and care for the environment.

At the core of Green Witchcraft is the belief in the healing and transformative power of nature. Modern Green Witches work with plants, herbs, crystals, and other natural materials to address physical, emotional, and spiritual challenges. By tapping into the wisdom of the Earth and harnessing the energies of the natural world, Green Witches foster healing, growth, and transformation within themselves and their communities.

In addition to using natural remedies, many Green Witches engage in practices that help them develop a deeper connection to the Earth. Activities such as gardening, nature walks, and meditation allow practitioners to attune themselves to the rhythms of the natural world and cultivate a profound sense of belonging and interconnectedness.

Gaia

The history of Earth worship and nature magic dates back to the earliest human civilizations, with reverence for the Earth and its natural forces playing a central role in the spiritual beliefs and practices of many ancient cultures. From the earliest animistic traditions, which saw spirits and divine energies in all aspects of the natural world, to the more formalized religious practices of later civilizations, the worship of the Earth and its cycles has been a constant theme throughout human history.

The concept of Gaia has its roots in ancient Greek mythology. Gaia was considered the primordial Earth goddess and the mother of all life. She was believed to have given birth to the sky, the mountains, and the seas, as well as the gods and goddesses who inhabited them. The worship of Gaia was widespread in the ancient world, with numerous shrines and temples dedicated to her veneration.

The development of goddess worship can be traced back to the prehistoric period when many early human societies held a deep reverence for the divine feminine. This reverence is evident in the many examples of ancient figurines and sculptures depicting female figures, often referred to as Venus figurines or Earth mothers. These figures are believed to represent the goddess in her various aspects, such as fertility, abundance, and the cycles of life and death.

As human societies evolved and became more complex, so too did the forms of goddess worship. In ancient Mesopotamia, the Sumerians revered the goddess Inanna, who was associated with love, fertility, and war. In Egypt, the goddess Isis was venerated as the ideal mother and wife, as well as the patroness of nature and magic. In the Celtic tradition, the goddess Brigid was honored as a deity of healing, poetry, and smithcraft, embodying the creative and nurturing aspects of the divine feminine.

Throughout history, goddess worship has been closely tied to the worship of the Earth and the cycles of nature. This connection can be seen in the many festivals and rituals dedicated to the goddess and her various aspects, often held at key points in the agricultural calendar. These celebrations, such as the ancient Greek Thesmophoria or the Roman festival of Ceres, were designed to honor the goddess and ensure the fertility of the land and the abundance of the harvest.

In the modern era, the worship of the Earth and the divine feminine has experienced a resurgence, with many contemporary spiritual traditions and paths incorporating elements of goddess worship and nature magic into their practices. Wicca, for example, is a nature-based religion that honors the goddess and the god as equal partners in the creation and maintenance of the world. The goddess is often seen as the embodiment of the Earth, with her changing aspects reflecting the cycles of nature and the passage of time.

Modern goddess worship also finds expression in the feminist spirituality movement, which seeks to reclaim the divine feminine as a source of empowerment and inspiration for women and men alike. This movement has led to a renewed interest in the ancient goddess traditions and the development of new rituals and practices designed to honor the Earth and the divine feminine.

Connecting to Mother Earth

Connecting with mother earth, or the natural world, can have profound benefits for our physical, mental, and spiritual wellbeing. In a world that often prioritizes technology and material possessions over our connection to the natural world, it is more important than ever to find ways to cultivate a deeper relationship with the earth. Here are some ways that we can connect with mother earth and experience the many benefits that come with it.

First, spending time in nature is one of the most direct ways to connect with mother earth. This could mean taking a walk in the woods, sitting by a stream or the ocean, or simply spending time in a local park. Being in nature can help us to feel more grounded, calm, and centered, and can provide a much-needed break from the stresses and distractions of modern life.

Another way to connect with mother earth is through gardening or farming. Growing your own food or tending to plants can help you to develop a deeper appreciation for the natural world and the cycles of life and death that underlie it. This can also help to foster a sense of responsibility and care for the earth, as we come to understand the interconnectedness of all living things.

Meditation and mindfulness practices can also be powerful tools for connecting with mother earth. By quieting the mind and focusing on our breath, we can begin to cultivate a deeper awareness of our surroundings and a sense of connection to the natural world. Mindfulness practices can also help to reduce stress and anxiety, promote emotional balance, and improve our overall sense of wellbeing.

Connecting with animals can also be a powerful way to connect with mother earth. Whether we have pets at home or simply enjoy watching the birds and other creatures in our local environment, animals can help us to feel more connected to the natural world and to develop a deeper sense of empathy and compassion for all living beings.

Participating in rituals and ceremonies that honor the natural world can be a powerful way to connect with mother earth. This could include practices such as smudging, drumming, or singing, which can help to create a sense of connection and harmony between us and the natural world.

There are many ways that we can connect with mother earth and experience the many benefits that come with it. By spending time in nature, practicing mindfulness, gardening, or farming, connecting with animals, and participating in rituals and ceremonies, we can begin to develop a deeper sense of connection to the natural world and to cultivate a more sustainable and harmonious relationship with our environment.

The ways I have consistently connected with Mother Earth include immersing myself in the outdoors, even if it's merely sitting on the porch. I find solace in experiencing the moments just before a storm. I cherish warm summer days spent with friends as we hike through trails, counting mushrooms and admiring the stunning waterfalls we encounter. We encourage one another to swim out to towering rock formations and daringly leap off rope swings into the river's depths. Together, we explore the creeks feeding the river, wading through shallow waters while seeking crawdads and minnows. I find myself swimming beneath cascading waterfalls that flow from mountain cliffs, savoring the refreshing mist on my face and the powerful surge of water surrounding me.

My bond with Mother Earth extends beyond exploration and swimming. I forage for wild berries and fruits, discovering succulent blackberries and plump blueberries concealed within the bushes near the forest's edge. I cultivate my own greens, herbs, and vegetables, too. My daughters and I delight in frolicking on nature's lush, mossy carpet, creating mud pies and potions from the clay and other natural treasures we find. We combine leaves, flowers, rocks, and dirt, assembling a mixture that's equally messy and enchanting. Our creations, though unique, share a commonality—a profound connection to the earth and its innate rhythms.

I strive to instill in my daughters a deep bond with Mother Earth, ensuring that it remains with them wherever life leads. When they venture off to college or begin working in the city, I hope they cultivate a small herb garden on their apartment balcony, dedicating time to nurturing the plants and observing their growth. I envision them taking leisurely strolls in nearby parks, feeling the grass underfoot and the sun's warmth on their faces. I hope they continue crafting mud pies and potions, unafraid of getting a little dirt beneath their fingernails.

Connecting with nature is not just going outside and touching grass, but it is a way of life. Connected to the natural world, you can find peace and comfort, and a sense of belonging that can be hard to find in the hustle and bustle of the modern world. We must continue to explore, to grow, and to create, knowing that She is there to guide and support us along the way.

Embracing and Harnessing your Power

To fully embrace one's power as a practitioner of green magic, it is essential to cultivate a deep connection with the natural world and develop an understanding of the energies and forces that permeate it. As green witches, we recognize that the Earth is a living, breathing entity, and that by tapping into its energies, we can harness the power to heal, transform, and manifest our desires.

Developing a relationship with the elements is a fundamental aspect of green witchcraft. By exploring the properties and energies associated with earth, air, fire, and water, we can develop a greater understanding of the forces that shape our world and learn to work with them in our magical practice. This elemental connection allows us to harness the power of nature to bring about positive change in our lives and the world around us.

One of the essential skills for a green witch is the ability to work with plants and herbs, which are at the heart of green magic. By cultivating a deep knowledge of the properties and uses of various plants, we can create powerful herbal remedies, magical potions, and spells that draw upon the Earth's healing energies. This knowledge also extends to the ethical and sustainable harvesting of plants, ensuring that we maintain a harmonious relationship with the natural world as we harness its power.

Connecting with the cycles of the Earth, such as the changing seasons, lunar phases, and solar cycles, is another crucial aspect of green witchcraft. By aligning our magical practice with these natural rhythms, we can tap into the ebb and flow of energies that underpin the Earth's cycles. This alignment allows us to work in harmony with the natural world, enhancing the effectiveness of our magic and ensuring that we are attuned to the energies that surround us.

To harness your power as a green witch, it is essential to develop a strong foundation in magical practice, rooted in the principles of your path. This can include cultivating a daily practice that may involve meditation, grounding exercises, or rituals designed to connect you with the Earth and its energies. By regularly engaging in these practices, you will build a strong energetic foundation upon which to build your magical skills and abilities.

Another important aspect of harnessing your power as a green witch is to develop a personal relationship with the spirits and energies of the natural world. This may involve working with plant spirits, elementals, or other nature-based entities that can offer guidance, wisdom, and support in your magical practice. By forging these connections, you open yourself to a deeper understanding of the natural world and its mysteries, enhancing your ability to work with its energies and manifest your intentions.

To truly harness your power as a green witch, it is also important to cultivate self-awareness and introspection. This involves examining your motivations, intentions, and desires, ensuring that your magical practice is aligned with your highest good and the greater good of all beings. By engaging in regular self-reflection and spiritual growth, you will ensure that your practice is grounded in love, compassion, and a desire to heal and transform both yourself and the world around you.

Finally, one of the most powerful ways to harness your power as a green witch is to share your knowledge and wisdom with others. By teaching, mentoring, and supporting others in their magical journey, you not only empower them to embrace their own gifts and abilities, but you also strengthen your own understanding and mastery of green magic. This sharing of wisdom and experience serves to create a vibrant, supportive community of green witches who are dedicated to healing, transformation, and the betterment of the world.

Concepts and Symbolism

The Elements

The Elements – Earth, Air, Fire, and Water – are fundamental to the practice of green magic and nature-based spirituality. These primal forces represent the building blocks of the universe, and by working with them, practitioners can harness their energies to achieve balance, harmony, and transformation. Each element corresponds to specific aspects of life and consciousness, and by understanding their unique qualities, we can better integrate them into our spiritual practice.

Earth, as the first element, represents the foundation upon which all life is built. It is associated with stability, grounding, and nourishment. In green magic, the Earth element is often linked to the physical realm, including the body, our connection to the natural world, and the manifestation of material abundance. Practitioners may work with the Earth element to promote growth, both in their gardens and their personal lives, or to cultivate a deeper sense of rootedness and connection to the planet. Some ways to connect with the Earth element include gardening, working with crystals and stones, or practicing grounding meditation techniques.

Air, the second element, symbolizes intellect, communication, and inspiration. In green magic, the Air element is connected to the realm of ideas, thoughts, and the power of the spoken and written word. By working with Air, practitioners can enhance their creative expression, sharpen their intuition, and foster clearer communication with themselves, others, and the natural world. To connect with the Air element, one might engage in activities such as journaling, deep breathing exercises, or spending time outdoors in the wind.

Fire, the third element, embodies transformation, passion, and energy. Within the practice of green magic, the Fire element is associated with the purifying and transformative power of the sun, as well as our inner drive and motivation. By working with Fire, practitioners can ignite their passions, clear away obstacles, and harness the energy needed to manifest their desires. Some ways to connect with the Fire element include candle magic, bonfires, or engaging in activities that inspire enthusiasm and excitement.

Water, the fourth element, represents emotions, intuition, and healing. In green magic, the Water element is connected to the realm of feelings, dreams, and the subconscious mind. By working with Water, practitioners can access their innate wisdom, foster emotional balance, and promote healing on a deep, soul level. To connect with the Water element, one might engage in activities such as taking ritual baths, working with the moon cycles, or spending time near bodies of water like rivers, lakes, or the ocean.

The concept of "Spirit," also known as "Aether" or "Akasha" in some traditions, is often considered the fifth element in many spiritual practices, including green magic and nature-based spirituality. This ethereal and elusive element transcends the tangible realm of the other four elements, representing the unifying force that binds them together and the divine essence that pervades all things.

Unlike the more tangible elements of Earth, Air, Fire, and Water, Spirit is not directly associated with a specific aspect of the physical world. Instead, it represents the underlying energy that connects all things, the vital force that animates life and fuels the universe. In this sense, Spirit can be seen as the cosmic glue that unites the four elements and serves as a bridge between the material and the spiritual realms.

In the context of green magic, the element of Spirit is particularly significant, as it reflects the deeper connection between the practitioner and the natural world, as well as the innate wisdom and sacred energy that flow through all living beings. By working with Spirit, green witches can tap into the divine essence that permeates the universe and strengthen their connection to the Source or the Divine, depending on their individual beliefs.

Some ways to connect with the element of Spirit might include meditation, prayer, or contemplative practices that focus on the interconnectedness of all things and the divine energy that flows through the web of life. Practitioners may also incorporate the concept of Spirit into their rituals and spells, using it as a unifying force to bring the energies of the other four elements into harmony and balance.

In addition to its role as a unifying force, Spirit is often associated with personal transformation and spiritual growth. By working with the element of Spirit, green witches can access their higher selves, cultivate a deeper understanding of their purpose and place in the world, and awaken their intuitive abilities. The practice of green magic with an emphasis on the element of Spirit can be a powerful catalyst for self-discovery, healing, and spiritual evolution.

Each element has its own unique energy, and by incorporating th elements into one's practice, a green witch can create a balanced and harmonious connection to the natural world. This balance can be achieved through various means, including the creation of elemental altars or sacred spaces, the use of elemental correspondences in rituals and spells, and the practice of meditation and visualization techniques that focus on the qualities of each element.

One important aspect of working with the elements is the recognition that they are interconnected and interdependent. Just as the natural world relies on the intricate balance of these elemental forces, so too must a green witch cultivate a deep understanding of their interplay in order to fully harness their power. By honoring and respecting the elements, practitioners can develop a holistic approach to their spiritual practice that acknowledges the interconnectedness of all life.

The Sun, Moon, and Stars

The Sun, the Moon, and the Stars have held great significance in various cultures and spiritual practices throughout history. Their celestial presence and the rhythms they create have a profound impact on the natural world, and as such, they can play an important role in nature-based spiritual practices, including green magic and witchcraft.

The Sun, as the primary source of light and energy for our planet, represents life, vitality, and growth. Its daily cycle influences our natural circadian rhythms, while its seasonal changes impact the earth's climate and the cycles of plant and animal life. In green magic, the Sun can be seen as a symbol of power, creativity, and transformation, and can be incorporated into rituals and spells focused on personal development, healing, and manifestation. Solar energy can also be harnessed in practical ways, such as through the use of solar-powered tools or by working with sun-loving plants in the garden.

The Moon, with its waxing and waning phases, embodies the cyclical nature of life and the constant interplay between light and darkness. Its gravitational pull affects the tides, and its cycles have long been associated with fertility, intuition, and emotional wellbeing. In nature-based spiritual practices, the Moon is often honored through rituals and ceremonies that align with its phases, such as the New Moon, Full Moon, and Dark Moon. By working with lunar energy, green witches can tap into the Moon's nurturing and transformative power, using it for self-reflection, emotional healing, and manifestation of intentions. Additionally, many practitioners choose to plant, harvest, and perform other garden tasks in accordance with the lunar cycles to harness the Moon's influence on plant growth.

The Stars, as distant celestial bodies, represent the vastness of the universe and the mysteries of the cosmos. They have served as navigational guides for travelers and have inspired countless myths and legends throughout human history. In nature-based spirituality, the Stars can symbolize guidance, wisdom, and the interconnectedness of all things. By observing the patterns and movements of the stars, green witches can develop a deeper understanding of the cosmic forces at play and how they influence the natural world. Star energy can be incorporated into rituals and spells focused on gaining clarity, seeking guidance, or connecting with ancestral wisdom. Stargazing or working with celestial charts can also be a meditative and grounding practice, providing a sense of perspective and awe at the vastness of the universe.

Sacred Shapes

Sacred shapes and geometry have been an integral part of human spirituality, mysticism, and witchcraft for thousands of years. These shapes, which can be found in nature and the cosmos, hold deep symbolic meaning and are believed to possess a powerful energy that can be harnessed in various magical practices. By understanding and working with these sacred forms, practitioners can tap into the universal wisdom and divine order that they embody, enhancing their spiritual work and personal growth.

One of the most well-known sacred shapes is the circle, representing wholeness, unity, and the cyclical nature of life. Circles can be found in the natural world, such as in the orbits of celestial bodies, the shape of fruits and flowers, and the ripples created by a drop of water. In witchcraft, the circle is often used to create sacred space during rituals and to contain and direct energy. Drawing or visualizing a circle can be a powerful way to protect oneself, focus one's intention, and connect with the energies of the universe.

Another significant sacred shape is the spiral, symbolizing growth, transformation, and the unfolding of life's mysteries. Spirals can be observed in the growth patterns of plants, the structure of galaxies, and the path of a winding river. In magical practices, the spiral can be used to help practitioners attune to the natural flow of energy and embrace the cycles of change that are inherent in life. Incorporating spirals into rituals, spells, and personal talismans can serve as a reminder of the interconnectedness of all things and the ongoing process of growth and evolution.

The hexagon, a six-sided shape often associated with the structure of honeycomb, represents harmony, balance, and the union of opposites. This shape is found in various natural phenomena, such as the arrangement of atoms in a crystal lattice and the pattern of a turtle's shell. In witchcraft, the hexagon can be used to symbolize the merging of polarities, such as light and darkness, masculine and feminine, or the physical and spiritual realms. Working with hexagonal patterns can help practitioners find balance in their lives and strengthen their connection to the energies of the universe.

The pentagram and pentacle are particularly significant symbols in the world of witchcraft and hold a special place within sacred geometry. The pentagram, a five-pointed star, represents the five classical elements of earth, air, fire, water, and spirit, and signifies the interconnectedness and balance of these forces. The pentacle, a pentagram enclosed in a circle, serves as a symbol of protection and is often used to invoke the energies of the elements during rituals. The circle that surrounds the star represents the unity and wholeness of all things, as well as the boundary between the physical and spiritual realms. Utilizing the pentagram and pentacle in magical practices can help practitioners to harness the power of the elements, maintain balance in their lives, and create a protective shield against negative energies.

Sacred geometry also includes more complex shapes, such as the Flower of Life, a pattern of overlapping circles that forms a flower-like design. This ancient symbol is believed to represent the interconnectedness of all living things and the underlying structure of the cosmos. Incorporating the Flower of Life into magical work can help practitioners tap into the universal energy that flows through all of creation, fostering a sense of unity and harmony with the natural world.

By studying and working with sacred shapes and geometry, practitioners of witchcraft can deepen their understanding of the patterns that govern the universe and the energies that shape their lives. Integrating these sacred forms into rituals, spells, and personal talismans can enhance the power and effectiveness of magical work, as well as foster a stronger connection to the natural world and the divine wisdom it embodies.

Seasons and Sabbats

The changing seasons have long held a central place in the beliefs and practices of earth-based spiritual traditions, including green magic and paganism. As the earth's cycle progresses through the year, the shifting patterns of light, temperature, and life offer potent symbols of growth, transformation, and renewal. By attuning to the energies of each season and observing the associated equinoxes and sabbats, practitioners of green magic can deepen their connection to the natural world and harness the unique qualities of each season to support their spiritual journey.

The spring season, marked by the Spring Equinox (also known as Ostara), is a time of rebirth, renewal, and new beginnings. As the days grow longer and the earth begins to awaken from its winter slumber, life returns to the land in the form of budding plants, blossoming flowers, and the arrival of young animals. This season offers a powerful opportunity for practitioners to embrace new possibilities, set intentions for personal growth, and engage in practices that support creativity and fertility. Celebrating the Spring Equinox can involve rituals and activities such as planting seeds, both literally and metaphorically, to symbolize the growth and transformation that the season brings.

The summer season, commencing with the Summer Solstice (or Litha), is a time of abundance, vitality, and celebration. As the sun reaches its peak in the sky, the earth is bathed in warmth and light, fostering growth and maturation in the natural world. This season invites practitioners to tap into their own inner fire, harnessing the energy of the sun to fuel their passions and ambitions. The Summer Solstice can be observed through rituals that honor the sun's power, such as lighting a bonfire or engaging in solar meditations, as well as through activities that celebrate the abundance of the season, such as harvesting and sharing fresh produce.

The autumn season, heralded by the Autumn Equinox (or Mabon), is a time of balance, introspection, and gratitude. As the days grow shorter and the earth begins to prepare for the winter months ahead, the focus shifts from growth and expansion to reflection and release. This season encourages practitioners to take stock of their achievements and lessons learned throughout the year, expressing gratitude for the blessings in their lives and letting go of anything that no longer serves them. Celebrating the Autumn Equinox may involve rituals that honor the balance of light and dark, such as creating an altar with symbols of both, as well as activities that emphasize gratitude and sharing, such as participating in a harvest feast with loved ones.

The winter season, which begins with the Winter Solstice (or Yule), is a time of stillness, rest, and introspection. As the earth is cloaked in darkness and cold, life retreats inward, offering an opportunity for reflection, healing, and regeneration. This season invites practitioners to embrace the quietude and solitude of the darker months, turning inward to examine their inner landscape and tend to their emotional and spiritual needs. The Winter Solstice can be observed through rituals that honor the return of the light, such as lighting candles or a Yule log, as well as through activities that foster inner warmth and connection, such as gathering with loved ones to share stories and offer support.

The progression of the seasons offers a powerful framework for understanding and engaging with the cycles of the earth and the patterns of life. By attuning to the energies of each season and celebrating the equinoxes and sabbats that mark their transitions, practitioners of green magic can cultivate a deeper connection with the natural world and align their spiritual practice with the rhythms of the earth. Through this alignment, they can more fully embody the principles of balance, interconnectedness, and reverence for the earth that underpin their nature-based spirituality.

Trees

Trees have held a significant place in the spiritual and magical practices of numerous cultures and traditions throughout history, including those of green witchcraft and nature-based spirituality. Revered for their strength, resilience, and longevity, trees serve as potent symbols of wisdom, growth, and the interconnectedness of all life. As practitioners of green magic, we can form meaningful connections with trees and harness their unique energies and properties to enhance our spiritual practice.

One way to engage with the energies of trees is through the practice of tree meditation, where a practitioner attunes to the presence of a specific tree, sensing its energy and establishing a connection with the tree spirit. By sitting or standing near the tree, touching its trunk or branches, and focusing one's awareness on the tree's presence, a practitioner can deepen their bond with the tree and gain insights into its unique wisdom and energy. This practice not only fosters a greater appreciation for the natural world but also serves as a powerful tool for grounding, centering, and healing.

Trees also possess distinctive magical properties, which can be harnessed through the use of their leaves, bark, wood, and other parts in spells and rituals. For example, oak trees are associated with strength, protection, and stability, while willow trees are linked to intuition, emotional healing, and the moon. By incorporating tree materials into one's magical workings, a practitioner can tap into the specific qualities and energies of the tree, enhancing the potency and focus of their intention. However, it is essential to harvest tree materials ethically and respectfully, with gratitude and awareness of the tree's needs and boundaries.

Moreover, trees can serve as powerful allies and teachers in one's spiritual journey. By forming relationships with different tree species, a practitioner can learn from their unique wisdom and embody their qualities in their own life. For instance, the resilience of a pine tree in harsh conditions can inspire one to persevere through challenges, while the graceful flexibility of a birch tree can teach the importance of adaptability and fluidity. Building connections with tree spirits can also facilitate communication with other nature spirits and elemental beings, further enriching one's spiritual practice.

In addition to their magical and spiritual properties, trees play a crucial role in the physical and energetic health of the planet. They purify the air, provide habitat for countless species, and contribute to the balance and stability of ecosystems. As practitioners of green magic, we can honor and support trees through our actions, such as planting new trees, engaging in conservation efforts, and advocating for policies that protect and preserve forests and other natural habitats. By doing so, we not only deepen our own connection with the natural world but also contribute to the wellbeing of the earth and all its inhabitants.

Flowers

In green witchcraft and element work, flowers are often associated with the element of air and are seen as powerful tools for promoting healing, transformation, and spiritual growth. Flowers are considered to be vessels of the earth's energy and can be used to connect with the natural world, as well as with higher spiritual realms.

One of the key principles of green witchcraft is the idea that all living things are connected, and that by working with the energies of nature, we can promote balance, harmony, and well-being in our own lives and in the world around us. Flowers, with their delicate beauty and powerful energies, can help us to tap into the natural world and to connect with the spiritual energies that flow through all living things.

In element work, flowers are often associated with the element of air, which is associated with communication, creativity, and the power of the mind. Working with flowers can help to promote clarity of thought, inspire creativity, and enhance our ability to communicate with others and with the spiritual realm.

Flowers can be used in a variety of ways in green witchcraft and element work. For example, they can be used in meditation and ritual work, as well as in divination and spiritual guidance. They can also be used in herbal remedies and in the creation of magical oils, tinctures, and other preparations.

The power of flowers in green witchcraft and element work lies in their ability to connect us with the natural world and with higher spiritual realms. By working with the energies of flowers, we can tap into the transformative power of nature and promote healing, growth, and transformation in our own lives and in the world around us.

The Magical Properties of Flowers

Flowers have been used for centuries for their magical and healing properties. Their vibrant colors and fragrances have been utilized to help people heal, find love, and connect with the natural world. Flowers were used in ancient medicine as early as Sanskrit writings, and many modern pharmaceuticals were originally derived from plants, and the mystical properties of flowers.

The use of flowers for medicinal purposes dates back to ancient times. The Ayurvedic system of medicine, which originated in India more than 5,000 years ago, mentions the use of flowers in its Sanskrit writings. The Egyptians also used flowers such as chamomile, lotus, and lilies for their healing properties. In traditional Chinese medicine, the chrysanthemum flower has been used for centuries to treat respiratory illnesses and high blood pressure.

The Greeks and Romans also recognized the importance of flowers in medicine. The famous Greek physician Hippocrates, known as the father of modern medicine, used flowers such as poppies and crocuses to treat pain and inflammation. The Romans, on the other hand, used lavender and rosemary to relieve stress and anxiety.

Many modern pharmaceuticals were originally derived from plants. For example, aspirin was originally derived from the bark of willow trees, and the heart medication digoxin was derived from the foxglove plant. In fact, around 40% of all modern pharmaceuticals are based on natural substances found in plants.

Flowers are often used for their healing properties. Chamomile, for example, is known for its calming and relaxing properties and is often used to treat anxiety and insomnia. Lavender is also a popular herb used to relieve stress and promote relaxation. Calendula is another flower often used in herbalism to heal skin irritations and wounds.

In green witchcraft, flowers are believed to possess mystical properties that can be harnessed for magical purposes. Each flower is associated with a particular energy or intention, and can be used to cast spells, make potions, and perform rituals. For example, roses are often associated with love and passion, while lavender is believed to have a calming and cleansing effect.

Flowers have been used for centuries for their magical and healing properties. From ancient civilizations to modern medicine, the power of flowers has been recognized and utilized for their medicinal properties. The use of flowers in green witchcraft has not only helped people heal but has also connected them to the natural world and the mystical energies that exist within it.

Magical Properties of Commonly Used Flowers

Angelica (Angelica archangelica): Angelica is used for protection, healing, and spiritual connection. Its flowers and leaves can be added to incense, teas, and baths for enhancing angelic communication, promoting emotional healing, and warding off negativity. Angelica is also believed to provide strength and courage during challenging times.

Anemone (Anemone spp.): Anemones symbolize protection and healing. Their flowers can be incorporated into spells for emotional healing, warding off negativity, and promoting a sense of inner peace. In ancient times, anemones were often planted around homes to protect against evil spirits and negative energies.

Belladonna (Atropa belladonna): Belladonna, also known as deadly nightshade, is associated with transformation, rebirth, and psychic abilities. Caution is advised when using belladonna, as it is highly toxic. It can be incorporated into spells for personal transformation, enhancing psychic visions, and connecting with darker aspects of the self. Historically, belladonna has been used in various magical practices, including flying ointments and potions.

Bluebell (Hyacinthoides non-scripta): Bluebells are used for protection, communication, and clarity. They can be incorporated into rituals for enhancing psychic abilities, improving communication, and dispelling confusion. Bluebells are also believed to attract faeries and create a connection to the magical realms.

Calendula (Calendula officinalis): Calendula is known for its healing and protective properties. Its petals can be used in spells for physical and emotional healing, as well as for protection against negative energies. Calendula is also associated with the sun and can be used to invoke solar energies in rituals.

Chamomile (Matricaria chamomilla): This flower is commonly used for relaxation, tranquility, and protection. It is often added to herbal teas, baths, and pouches for sleep and meditation, and can be used in spells to attract luck and prosperity. Chamomile is also associated with purification and has been used in ancient cultures for spiritual cleansing.

Daffodil (Narcissus spp.): Daffodils symbolize new beginnings, rebirth, and inspiration. They can be used in spells for personal growth, creativity, and embracing change. In folklore, daffodils were believed to provide protection and guidance, often planted near doorways to ward off negativity.

Daisy (Bellis perennis): Daisies are associated with innocence, purity, and love. They can be used in spells for attracting love, promoting self-love, and enhancing spiritual connections. Daisies are also believed to aid in healing emotional wounds and encouraging a positive outlook on life.

Dandelion (Taraxacum officinale): Dandelions are often used in spells related to wishes, desires, and manifestation. Their seeds can be blown into the wind with a specific intention or added to sachets and charm bags for good luck and prosperity. Dandelions have strong associations with the element of air, making them useful in spells for communication and mental clarity.

Elderflower (Sambucus nigra): Elderflowers are used for protection, banishing, and transformation. They can be used in rituals to protect a space, person, or object, and are often added to magical concoctions for personal transformation and spiritual growth. In European folklore, elder trees were considered sacred and believed to house powerful spirits.

Forget-me-not (Myosotis spp.): Forget-me-nots are used for remembrance, love, and friendship. They can be incorporated into spells for strengthening bonds, remembering past lives, and healing emotional wounds. Forget-me-nots are also associated with loyalty and maintaining connections with loved ones who have passed away.

Foxglove (Digitalis purpurea): Foxglove is associated with protection, healing, and inner growth. It is highly toxic, so caution must be exercised when using it. It can be used in spells for shielding against negativity, promoting emotional healing, and encouraging self-discovery. In folklore, foxglove is believed to be connected to the faerie realm, and its flowers can be used to communicate with faeries.

Heather (Calluna vulgaris): Heather is associated with attraction, passion, and good luck. Its flowers can be used in love spells, rituals for enhancing relationships, and for attracting good fortune. Heather is also thought to aid in spiritual development and communication with spirits.

Hibiscus (Hibiscus spp.): Hibiscus is used for love, divination, and dream work. Its flowers can be added to love potions, incense, and herbal blends for increasing passion and promoting prophetic dreams. Hibiscus is also thought to have protective properties, making it useful in warding off negativity and evil influences.

Honeysuckle (Lonicera spp.): Honeysuckle is used for love, attraction, and prosperity. Its flowers can be added to love potions, incense, and candles for attracting romance, enhancing existing relationships, and promoting abundance. Honeysuckle is also associated with psychic awareness and intuition, making it useful for divination and dream work.

Jasmine (Jasminum officinale): Jasmine is frequently used in love and sensuality spells. Its flowers can be added to oils, incense, and candles to attract love, enhance romance, and promote self-confidence. Jasmine is also believed to aid in spiritual growth and help with prophetic dreaming.

Lavender (Lavandula angustifolia): Lavender is often used in spells for calming, peace, and protection. Its flowers can be burned as incense, added to sleep pillows, or used in rituals to cleanse spaces and ward off negative energies. Lavender is also associated with healing, making it useful in soothing emotional and physical pain.

Lily (Lilium spp.): Lilies are often used for purity, protection, and spiritual growth. They can be incorporated into rituals for cleansing, consecration, and connecting with higher realms or spirit guides. Lilies have a long history of use in funeral rites, symbolizing the soul's transition to the afterlife.

Marigold (Tagetes spp.): Marigolds symbolize protection, transformation, and regeneration. They can be used in spells for psychic protection, spiritual growth, and releasing negative energies. In some cultures, marigolds are believed to attract and appease ancestral spirits, making them a popular addition to altars and offerings.

Morning Glory (Ipomoea spp.): Morning glories symbolize new beginnings, hope, and spiritual awakening. They can be used in spells for personal transformation, embracing change, and connecting with higher realms. Morning glory seeds have been used in some cultures for their hallucinogenic properties, which were thought to aid in spiritual journeys and visions.

Orchid (Orchidaceae family): Orchids symbolize love, beauty, and sensuality. They can be used in spells for enhancing relationships, promoting self-confidence, and embracing inner beauty. Orchids are also associated with fertility, making them useful in spells and rituals for conception and childbirth.

Peony (Paeonia spp.): Peonies are used for protection, good luck, and prosperity. Their petals can be used in rituals for shielding against negativity, attracting Poppy (Papaver spp.): Poppies symbolize sleep, dreams, and fertility. They can be used in spells for enhancing dream work, promoting relaxation, and aiding in fertility rituals. Poppies have been used historically in various cultures for their calming and pain-relieving properties.

Rose (Rosa spp.): Roses are used for love spells, self-love, and emotional healing. Their petals can be added to love potions, bath rituals, and used in sachets to attract romance or enhance existing relationships. Roses are also associated with the divine feminine and can be used in rituals to connect with goddess energy.

Snapdragon (Antirrhinum majus): Snapdragons are associated with protection, transformation, and banishing negativity. They can be used in spells for warding off evil, releasing negative energies, and promoting personal growth. In some folklore, snapdragons were believed to protect against deceit and falsehood, making them useful in truth-seeking spells.

Sunflower (Helianthus annuus): Sunflowers symbolize strength, growth, and solar energy. They can be used in spells for success, abundance, and personal power, and are often incorporated into rituals honoring the sun. Sunflowers are also thought to help with mental clarity, making them useful in spells for concentration and focus.

Violet (Viola spp.): Violets are associated with love, protection, and spirituality. They can be used in spells for attracting love, warding off negative energies, and enhancing spiritual connections. Violets are also believed to aid in spiritual growth and have a long history of use in love potions and amulets.

Vervain (Verbena officinalis): Vervain is often used in spells for protection, purification, and healing. Its leaves and flowers can be added to charm bags, incense, and teas for spiritual cleansing, as well as for banishing negative energies and promoting a sense of peace. Vervain is also known for its associations with divine and supernatural forces, making it useful in rituals for invoking deities and communicating with spirits.

Yarrow (Achillea millefolium): Yarrow is used for protection, courage, and psychic abilities. Its flowers and leaves can be added to charm bags, teas, and incense for increasing intuition, enhancing psychic visions, and promoting bravery. Yarrow has a long history of medicinal use and is also believed to aid in strengthening personal boundaries and warding off energetic intrusions.

Healing Herbs

Herbs are another powerful tool in green witchcraft and element work. Herbs have been used for thousands of years in various forms of traditional medicine and spiritual practice and are often associated with the element of earth and the energy of grounding, stability, and nurturing.

In green witchcraft, herbs are used for a variety of purposes, including promoting physical and emotional healing, enhancing spiritual awareness, and connecting with the natural world. Herbs can be used in a variety of ways, such as in herbal remedies, teas, tinctures, and other preparations.

They can also be used in ritual work and meditation, as well as in divination and spiritual guidance.

One of the key principles of green witchcraft is the idea that all living things are connected, and that by working with the energies of nature, we can promote balance, harmony, and well-being in our own lives and in the world around us. Herbs, with their unique energies and properties, can help us to tap into the natural world and to connect with the spiritual energies that flow through all living things.

Herbs are often associated with specific spiritual properties and energies and can be used to promote specific intentions and outcomes. For example, lavender is often used to promote relaxation and to relieve stress, while rosemary is often used to enhance memory and mental clarity.

Ultimately, the power of herbs in green witchcraft and element work lies in their ability to connect us with the natural world and with higher spiritual realms. By working with the energies of herbs, we can tap into the transformative power of nature and promote healing, growth, and transformation in our own lives and in the world around us. The following is a list of commonly used herbs and the properties that are attributed to them.

Chamomile - Chamomile is known for its calming and relaxing properties. It is often used to promote sleep, reduce anxiety, and soothe digestive issues.

Echinacea - Echinacea is a powerful immune booster that is often used to prevent and treat colds and flu. It also has anti-inflammatory properties that can help with arthritis and other inflammatory conditions.

Lavender - Lavender is known for its calming and soothing properties. It is often used to promote relaxation, reduce stress and anxiety, and help with insomnia.

St. John's Wort - St. John's Wort is a natural antidepressant that can help to alleviate symptoms of depression and anxiety. It also has anti-inflammatory and antiviral properties.

Ginger - Ginger is a natural anti-inflammatory that can help with a variety of conditions, including arthritis, digestive issues, and menstrual cramps. It also has antimicrobial properties that can help to fight off infections.

Peppermint - Peppermint is known for its cooling and soothing properties. It can help to alleviate headaches, muscle pain, and digestive issues.

Turmeric - Turmeric is a powerful anti-inflammatory that can help with a variety of conditions, including arthritis, digestive issues, and skin conditions. It also has antioxidant properties that can help to protect against cellular damage.

Sage - Sage is a natural antiseptic that can help to fight off infections. It also has anti-inflammatory properties that can help with conditions such as arthritis and asthma.

Rosemary - Rosemary is known for its cognitive-enhancing properties. It can help to improve memory and mental clarity, and also has anti-inflammatory and antioxidant properties.

Aloe vera - Aloe vera is a natural anti-inflammatory that can help with a variety of skin conditions, including burns, eczema, and psoriasis. It also has antimicrobial properties that can help to fight off infections.

Valerian - Valerian is a natural sedative that can help to promote relaxation and alleviate anxiety and insomnia.

Calendula - Calendula is a natural anti-inflammatory that can help with skin irritations, including eczema and acne. It also has antiviral properties that can help to fight off infections.

Lemon balm - Lemon balm is known for its calming and relaxing properties. It can help to reduce stress and anxiety, and also has antiviral properties that can help to prevent and treat cold sores.

Milk thistle - Milk thistle is a natural liver detoxifier that can help to protect against liver damage and improve liver function. It also has anti-inflammatory properties that can help with conditions such as arthritis and eczema.

Yarrow - Yarrow is a natural pain reliever that can help with headaches, menstrual cramps, and other types of pain. It also has antibacterial properties that can help to fight off infections.

Elderberry - Elderberry is a natural immune booster that can help to prevent and treat colds and flu. It also has anti-inflammatory properties that can help with conditions such as arthritis.

Passionflower - Passionflower is a natural sedative that can help to promote relaxation and alleviate anxiety and insomnia.

Catnip - Catnip is a natural sedative that can help to promote relaxation and alleviate anxiety and insomnia. It also has anti-inflammatory properties that can help with conditions such as arthritis.

Licorice - Licorice is a natural anti-inflammatory that can help with conditions such as arthritis and digestive issues. It also has antiviral properties that can help to fight off infections.

Ashwagandha - Ashwagandha is an adaptogenic herb that can help to reduce stress and anxiety, improve mood, and boost energy levels. It also has anti-inflammatory properties that can help with conditions such as arthritis.

Dandelion - Dandelion is a natural diuretic that can help to reduce bloating and water retention. It also has anti-inflammatory properties that can help with conditions such as arthritis and digestive issues.

Black Cohosh - Black Cohosh is a natural remedy for menopause symptoms such as hot flashes, night sweats, and mood swings. It also has anti-inflammatory properties that can help with conditions such as rheumatoid arthritis.

Garlic - Garlic is a natural antibacterial and antiviral that can help to boost the immune system and fight off infections. It also has anti-inflammatory properties that can help with conditions such as osteoarthritis.

Hawthorn - Hawthorn is a natural remedy for heart health that can help to lower blood pressure and cholesterol levels. It also has antioxidant properties that can help to protect against cell damage.

Please note that this is not an exhaustive list, and the information provided is intended for educational purposes only. Always consult with a qualified healthcare practitioner before using any herbs or supplements for medicinal purposes.

Wood Wisdom

In element work, wood is often associated with the element of earth and is used for grounding and connecting with nature. Trees are seen as powerful symbols of stability, growth, and longevity, and working with wood can help to channel these energies.

One way to work with wood in element work is to incorporate wooden objects into your sacred space or altar. This could include wooden bowls, carvings, or statues, which can help to connect you with the energy of the earth. You may also wish to use wooden wands or staffs during ritual or meditation, as these can help to channel and direct energy.

In addition to physical objects, you can also work with the energy of specific trees and types of wood. Different woods are associated with different properties and energies, and choosing the right type of wood can help to enhance your connection to the earth and the energy you wish to work with.

For example, cedar is often associated with purification and protection, while oak is associated with strength and stability. Birch is associated with new beginnings and fresh starts, while willow is associated with intuition and emotional healing. By incorporating different woods into your element work, you can tailor your practice to meet your specific needs and intentions.

It's important to remember that working with wood in element work should always be done with respect and reverence for the natural world. When selecting wood for ritual or meditation, try to choose sustainably harvested or reclaimed wood, and always ask permission before taking wood from trees in the wild. By honoring the energy and power of the trees, we can deepen our connection to the earth and all its natural beauty.

Fruit

Throughout history, fruit has been regarded as a symbol of abundance, fertility, and prosperity, and it has long been believed to possess magical properties. Fruits, with their vibrant colors, enticing scents, and unique flavors, have been used in various cultures as offerings to deities, as well as in rituals, spells, and ceremonies. The significance of fruit in the spiritual and magical realm can be attributed to several factors, including their connection to the cycles of nature, their nourishing qualities, and the symbolism they hold.

Fruits are closely tied to the natural cycles of the earth, as they grow and ripen in harmony with the changing seasons. This connection to the rhythms of nature lends fruit a unique power, as they embody the life-giving energies of the earth and the divine force that nourishes all living beings. As a result, fruits have often been used in rituals and ceremonies aimed at promoting growth, abundance, and prosperity, as well as in spells for love, fertility, and renewal.

The nourishing properties of fruit also contribute to their magical significance. As sources of sustenance, they provide essential nutrients and energy for both the body and the spirit. In many cultures, fruit has been viewed as a gift from the divine, a symbol of the bounty and generosity of the gods. This sacred association makes fruit an ideal offering in rituals and ceremonies, as well as a powerful ingredient in spells and charms for attracting abundance, love, and good fortune.

In addition to their connection to the natural cycles and their nourishing qualities, the symbolism of fruit plays a significant role in their magical properties. Different fruits have been associated with various deities, elements, and energies, making them valuable tools for practitioners seeking to tap into specific powers and influences. For example, fruit with a strong scent or flavor may be used in spells and rituals related to passion, sensuality, or attraction, while those with a more subtle taste or aroma might be employed in workings focused on peace, tranquility, or emotional healing. The following list goes over the attributes of some commonly used fruits.

Apple (Malus domestica): Apples symbolize love, fertility, and wisdom. They are often used in love spells, rituals for enhancing knowledge, and for connecting with the divine. Apples are also associated with the divine feminine and can be used in rituals to honor goddesses and feminine energy.

Apricot (Prunus armeniaca): Apricots symbolize love, passion, and happiness. They can be used in spells for attracting romance, enhancing relationships, and promoting joy. In some cultures, apricots are also believed to bring good luck and prosperity.

Avocado (Persea americana): Avocados represent love, fertility, and beauty. They can be used in spells for attracting love, promoting self-love, and enhancing one's physical appearance. Avocados are also associated with abundance and can be used in rituals for attracting wealth and prosperity.

Banana (Musa spp.): Bananas symbolize fertility, abundance, and prosperity. They can be used in spells for enhancing fertility, promoting success, and attracting wealth. Bananas are also thought to aid in emotional healing and can be used in rituals for releasing negativity and emotional baggage.

Blackberry (Rubus spp.): Blackberries represent protection, healing, and abundance. They can be used in spells for warding off negative energies, promoting physical and emotional healing, and attracting prosperity. Blackberries are also associated with the element of water and can be used in rituals for emotional balance and intuition.

Cherry (Prunus spp.): Cherries symbolize love, desire, and sensuality. They can be used in spells for attracting romance, enhancing passion, and deepening emotional connections. Cherries are also thought to promote self-confidence and personal power, making them useful in spells for empowerment and success.

Coconut (Cocos nucifera): Coconuts represent protection, purification, and spiritual growth. They can be used in spells for cleansing negative energies, promoting spiritual development, and strengthening personal boundaries. Coconuts are also associated with the moon and can be used in rituals honoring lunar deities and energies.

Fig (Ficus carica): Figs symbolize fertility, abundance, and wisdom. They can be used in spells for enhancing fertility, promoting intellectual growth, and attracting wealth. Figs are also thought to aid in emotional healing and can be used in rituals for releasing emotional blockages and promoting self-love.

Grape (Vitis spp.): Grapes represent abundance, fertility, and transformation. They can be used in spells for attracting prosperity, enhancing fertility, and promoting personal growth. Grapes are also associated with the process of fermentation and can be used in rituals for transformation and spiritual development.

Lemon (Citrus limon): Lemons symbolize purification, clarity, and protection. They can be used in spells for cleansing negative energies, promoting mental clarity, and warding off negativity. Lemons are also associated with the element of air and can be used in rituals for communication and creativity.

Mango (Mangifera indica): Mangoes represent love, abundance, and spiritual growth. They can be used in spells for attracting love, promoting prosperity, and enhancing spiritual development. Mangoes are also thought to aid in emotional healing and can be used in rituals for releasing negativity and embracing self-love.

Orange (Citrus sinensis): Oranges symbolize love, joy, and abundance. They can be used in spells for attracting romance, promoting happiness, and attracting wealth. Oranges are also associated with solar energies and can be used in rituals for empowerment, confidence, and success.

Papaya (Carica papaya): Papayas represent love, protection, and healing Peach (Prunus persica): Peaches symbolize love, happiness, and longevity. They can be used in spells for attracting romance, promoting joy, and enhancing vitality. In Chinese culture, peaches are believed to bring good fortune and are often used in rituals for attracting luck and prosperity.

Pear (Pyrus communis): Pears represent love, fertility, and wisdom. They can be used in spells for enhancing relationships, promoting intellectual growth, and attracting abundance. Pears are also associated with the divine feminine and can be used in rituals to connect with goddess energy and feminine wisdom.

Pineapple (Ananas comosus): Pineapples symbolize hospitality, abundance, and protection. They can be used in spells for attracting wealth, promoting friendship, and warding off negativity. Pineapples are also thought to aid in spiritual growth and can be used in rituals for personal transformation and spiritual development.

Plum (Prunus domestica): Plums represent love, protection, and intuition. They can be used in spells for attracting romance, warding off negative energies, and enhancing psychic abilities. Plums are also associated with the element of water and can be used in rituals for emotional balance and spiritual growth.

Pomegranate (Punica granatum): Pomegranates symbolize fertility, abundance, and transformation. They can be used in spells for enhancing fertility, attracting prosperity, and promoting personal growth. Pomegranates are also associated with the underworld and can be used in rituals for connecting with ancestors and exploring the mysteries of life and death.

Raspberry (Rubus idaeus): Raspberries represent love, protection, and fertility. They can be used in spells for attracting romance, warding off negative energies, and enhancing fertility. Raspberries are also thought to aid in emotional healing and can be used in rituals for releasing emotional pain and promoting self-love.

Strawberry (Fragaria spp.): Strawberries symbolize love, happiness, and sensuality. They can be used in spells for attracting romance, promoting joy, and enhancing passion. Strawberries are also associated with the element of earth and can be used in rituals for grounding, stability, and connecting with nature.

Always use caution when working with fruits and plants in your magical practice. Research their properties, ethical sources, and potential toxicities before use. Be aware of any allergies or sensitivities you or others may have to certain fruits or plants.

Essential Oils

Essential oils have been used for centuries for their therapeutic and medicinal properties. They are highly concentrated oils extracted from plants that have been distilled or cold-pressed. Each essential oil has a unique chemical composition that contributes to its specific aroma and benefits.

One of the most common uses of essential oils is in aromatherapy, which involves inhaling the scent of the oils to stimulate the brain and promote relaxation, focus, or other desired effects. Essential oils can also be applied topically or ingested, but it is important to do so safely and with caution.

When using essential oils, it is important to choose high-quality oils that have been properly stored and labeled. Essential oils should always be diluted with a carrier oil before being applied to the skin to avoid irritation or other adverse reactions.

Some popular essential oils and their uses include:

Lavender: known for its calming and relaxing properties, lavender can also be used to soothe skin irritations and promote restful sleep.

Peppermint: often used to alleviate headaches and improve digestion, peppermint is also energizing and can help improve focus and mental clarity.

Tea Tree: known for its antiseptic and anti-inflammatory properties, tea tree oil can be used to treat acne, dandruff, and other skin conditions.

Eucalyptus: often used to relieve congestion and respiratory issues, eucalyptus oil can also help reduce inflammation and ease muscle pain.

Lemon: known for its cleansing and uplifting properties, lemon oil can also be used to improve mood and boost energy levels.

Essential oils can be a powerful tool for improving physical and mental health when used safely and with knowledge of their properties and potential risks. It is important to do your research and consult with a healthcare professional before using essential oils, particularly if you have any medical conditions or are pregnant or breastfeeding.

Crystals and Stones

Crystals and stones have been used for centuries in various cultures and traditions for their unique energetic properties and their ability to amplify, store, and transmit energy. In witchcraft, they serve as powerful tools for harnessing and directing energy in rituals, spells, and daily practices. Their natural vibrational frequencies can help to balance and align our own energies, making them invaluable for energy work, meditation, and spiritual growth.

One common way to incorporate crystals and stones into witchcraft is by using them to create grids or layouts for specific intentions. By arranging stones in specific patterns, practitioners can amplify their energies, creating a powerful energetic field that can be used for manifestation, healing, or protection. Additionally, crystals and stones can be used as talismans or amulets, carrying their energetic properties with the practitioner and providing constant support and protection.

Another popular use for crystals and stones in witchcraft is in meditation and energy work. Holding or placing a crystal on a specific chakra or energy point can help to activate, cleanse, or balance the associated energies, promoting healing and overall wellbeing. Crystals can also be used to enhance psychic abilities, such as intuition, clairvoyance, or telepathy, by working with stones that resonate with the third eye or crown chakra.

In spellwork, crystals and stones can be used to amplify the energy of a spell or to represent specific intentions, such as love, prosperity, or protection. For example, one might place a rose quartz crystal in a love spell to attract romantic energy or use a piece of black tourmaline to ward off negative energies during a protection spell.

It is essential to cleanse and charge your crystals and stones regularly to maintain their energetic purity and potency. Cleansing can be done by smudging, burying in the earth, or placing them under moonlight or sunlight, while charging can be accomplished by placing them on a windowsill during a full moon or on a bed of selenite or quartz.

To discover the specific magical properties of various crystals and stones, refer to the correspondence section of this book. By understanding their unique qualities, you can choose the right crystal for your specific intention or purpose, harnessing their power to enhance and elevate your witchcraft practice.

Native Flora

The native flora plays a crucial role in the practice of green witchcraft, as it helps forge a strong bond with the natural world, the local ecosystem, and the unique energies that surround you. By working with native plants, you create a more meaningful and powerful connection to the land, which in turn enhances your magical practice and spiritual growth.

Understanding and utilizing the native flora in green witchcraft is a way to honor and respect the traditions and wisdom of the ancestors who lived in the area. These plants have been used for centuries for medicinal, spiritual, and magical purposes, and by incorporating them into your practice, you tap into an ancient lineage of knowledge. You also foster a connection to the cultural history of your region, which enriches your magical work and deepens your understanding of the forces that shape the land and its energies.

Working with native plants also promotes environmental awareness and sustainability. By using plants that are indigenous to your region, you contribute to the preservation of local ecosystems and the protection of native species. This approach encourages biodiversity and helps to maintain the balance and harmony of the natural world. Additionally, using native plants in your practice minimizes the environmental impact of transporting non-native plants from distant locations, reducing your ecological footprint.

Using native plants in your green witchcraft practice allows you to align your magical work with the natural cycles of your environment. Each region has its own unique climate, seasons, and plant life, and by working with the native flora, you can synchronize your rituals, spells, and energy work with these natural rhythms. This alignment helps to strengthen your magical intentions and increase the effectiveness of your practice.

To connect with the native flora, it's essential to educate yourself about the plants that grow in your area. Spend time in nature, observing and learning about the different species, their growth patterns, and their traditional uses in medicine, folklore, and magic. Join local plant identification or foraging groups, where you can learn from experienced practitioners and expand your knowledge of the native plants in your region. By cultivating a relationship with your local flora, you'll find that your green witchcraft practice becomes more potent, grounded, and in harmony with the natural world.

Native Fauna

The native fauna is a vital aspect of green witchcraft, as it helps create a profound connection with the living beings that share the same environment as you. By understanding and honoring the native fauna, you form a deeper appreciation for the intricate web of life and the unique energies that each species brings to your surroundings. This interconnectedness enhances your magical practice and contributes to your spiritual growth.

Recognizing and respecting the native fauna in green witchcraft is a way to acknowledge the intricate balance of the ecosystems in your area. Each animal species plays a specific role in maintaining the stability of the environment, and by incorporating them into your practice, you tap into the wisdom and power of the natural world. You also develop a connection to the energy and spirit of the animals, which can serve as guides, allies, and sources of inspiration in your magical work.

Working with native fauna encourages ecological mindfulness and ethical stewardship. By focusing on the animals indigenous to your region, you become more aware of their needs and the challenges they face, such as habitat loss, pollution, and climate change. This awareness can inspire you to engage in conservation efforts and adopt sustainable practices that protect and preserve native wildlife. By incorporating these principles into your green witchcraft practice, you demonstrate reverence for the natural world and contribute to its well-being.

Incorporating native fauna into your magical practice also allows you to align your work with the natural cycles and rhythms of the animal kingdom. Each region has its own distinct patterns of animal migration, reproduction, and behavior, and by attuning your rituals and spells to these rhythms, you create a more harmonious and powerful practice. This alignment helps to amplify your intentions and increase the effectiveness of your magical work.

To connect with the native fauna, it's essential to educate yourself about the animals that inhabit your area. Spend time in nature, observing and learning about the different species, their behaviors, and their roles in the local ecosystems. Attend workshops or join local wildlife groups, where you can learn from knowledgeable experts and share your experiences with other like-minded practitioners. By nurturing a relationship with your local fauna, you'll find that your green witchcraft practice becomes more vibrant, connected, and attuned to the living world that surrounds you.

Rivers, Lakes, and Streams

Rivers, lakes, streams, and other bodies of water have held a special place in the hearts of humans for millennia, often serving as the lifeblood of ancient civilizations and playing an essential role in the development of societies. They have long been revered in pagan practices and all incarnations of witchcraft and magic for their life-sustaining, purifying, and transformative properties. They symbolize the ever-changing nature of existence, as well as the constant flow of energy and emotions that shape our lives.

In many ancient pagan traditions, water was considered a sacred element, representing the divine feminine, fertility, and abundance. It was believed that rivers, lakes, and streams were inhabited by deities, nymphs, and other mystical beings, who provided protection, guidance, and blessings to those who honored them. Offerings were often made to these water spirits, in the form of flowers, fruits, and other tokens of gratitude, to ensure a harmonious relationship with the natural world and maintain the balance of the elements.

Rivers, in particular, have been the focus of various magical practices and rituals, symbolizing the passage of time, renewal, and the flow of life itself. They were often used for divination, as the movement of the water was believed to carry messages from the gods and reveal the secrets of the future. The healing properties of rivers were also celebrated, with people bathing in their waters to cleanse themselves of negative energies and restore their physical and spiritual well-being.

Lakes and ponds, with their still and reflective surfaces, represent the power of introspection and the ability to look within oneself for answers and guidance. They have been used in rituals to aid meditation and promote emotional healing, as well as to connect with the deeper wisdom and mysteries of the subconscious mind. The serene nature of lakes also makes them ideal for rites of passage, as they symbolize the transformative journey from one stage of life to another.

Streams, the smaller and more intimate waterways, offer unique opportunities for personal connection and communion with the element of water. They embody the interconnectedness of all living things, as they carry nutrients and energy from one place to another, fostering growth and nourishment throughout the ecosystem. In pagan practices, streams can be used for purification, blessings, and the casting of spells, as their flowing waters help to carry intentions and energies out into the world.

Ritual Work and Sacred Spaces

In the practice of Green Witchcraft and nature-based spirituality, ritual work and the creation of sacred spaces hold significant importance. These practices allow us to forge a deeper connection with the earth, the elements, and the energies that flow through the natural world. By engaging in rituals and designating sacred spaces, we align ourselves with the rhythms and cycles of nature, tapping into the inherent power and wisdom that exists within the earth and within ourselves.

Ritual work encompasses a wide range of practices, from simple daily rituals to more elaborate ceremonies that mark significant events or seasonal transitions. These rituals serve to bring focus and intention to our spiritual practice, helping us to attune our energies to the energies of the earth and the elements. By engaging in ritual work, we open ourselves to the flow of energy and inspiration, allowing us to draw on the power and wisdom of the natural world to support our personal growth and spiritual development.

Sacred spaces play a crucial role in facilitating our ritual work and providing a dedicated environment for spiritual practice. Whether it is a small altar in a corner of your home, a garden sanctuary, or a secluded spot in a nearby forest, creating a sacred space allows us to cultivate a sense of reverence and connection to the energies and spirits of the land. These spaces provide a sanctuary where we can retreat from the distractions and demands of daily life, immersing ourselves in the healing embrace of nature and reconnecting with our inner selves.

Both ritual work and sacred spaces are integral to the practice of Green Witchcraft, as they help us to develop a deeper, more profound relationship with the natural world and its energies. Through the creation of sacred spaces and the performance of ritual work, we can align ourselves with the cycles and rhythms of the earth, opening ourselves to the transformative power of nature and deepening our understanding of the interconnectedness of all life. In the following section, we will explore the many facets of ritual work and sacred spaces, offering guidance on how to incorporate these practices into your own spiritual journey and cultivate a stronger connection to the earth and its abundant wisdom.

Outdoor Spaces

Creating an outdoor sacred space in nature allows us to connect with the earth and the elements in a deeply personal and profound way. By designing a space that resonates with your unique spiritual path and practice, you can cultivate a sanctuary that allows you to immerse yourself in the healing and transformative power of nature.

To begin creating your outdoor sacred space, consider the location. Choose a spot that feels energetically aligned with your intentions and practice, whether it's a secluded corner of your garden, a quiet clearing in the woods, or a peaceful spot near a body of water. Take time to connect with the land and the spirits that dwell there and consider asking for their permission and guidance as you create your sacred space.

Incorporating representations of the elements is an essential aspect of designing an outdoor sacred space. Earth, air, fire, and water each hold unique energies and qualities, and by honoring and including them in your space, you can create a balanced and harmonious environment. For example, you might include a small bowl of soil or a stone to represent the earth, a feather or wind chime for air, a candle or fire pit for fire, and a bowl of water or a small fountain for water. By mindfully placing these representations in your space, you can create a powerful connection to the energies of the elements and the natural world.

As you design your outdoor sacred space, consider incorporating plants, flowers, and herbs that hold special significance to your practice. This might include plants that are associated with your patron deity, those that are known for their magical or healing properties, or simply those that you find beautiful and inspiring. By surrounding yourself with the living energy of these plants, you can create a vibrant and nurturing environment that supports your spiritual growth and connection to the earth.

Adding personal and meaningful touches to your outdoor sacred space can help you feel more connected and engaged with your practice. This might include incorporating symbols or artwork that resonate with your spiritual beliefs, creating an altar adorned with sacred objects, or using textiles or other decorative elements that hold special meaning for you. By customizing your space to reflect your unique spiritual path and preferences, you can create an environment that feels truly sacred and inspiring.

Remember that your outdoor sacred space is a living, evolving reflection of your spiritual journey. As you grow and change, your space can change with you, adapting to your needs and the shifting rhythms of the earth. Be open to the natural ebb and flow of energy in your space, and allow yourself the freedom to explore, experiment, and adapt as needed. By creating a sacred space that is uniquely your own, you can cultivate a deeper connection to the earth and the elements and experience the transformative power of nature in your spiritual practice.

Indoor Spaces

Creating an indoor sacred space offers a unique opportunity to bring the energy of nature into your home, allowing you to maintain a strong connection to the earth and the elements even when you are not able to venture outdoors. While the process of designing an indoor sacred space shares some similarities with creating an outdoor space, there are distinct considerations and challenges to keep in mind as you create your sanctuary within the confines of your home.

One of the first steps in creating an indoor sacred space is to choose a suitable location. Ideally, this should be a quiet, private area where you can focus on your spiritual practice without distractions. A dedicated room or a secluded corner in your living space can work well for this purpose. Ensure that the space is kept clean and clutter-free to encourage a sense of tranquility and focus.

As with an outdoor sacred space, incorporating representations of the elements is an essential aspect of designing an indoor sanctuary. Since you may not have the luxury of utilizing natural elements such as a fire pit or a water feature indoors, consider using more compact and symbolic representations. You might use a small dish of salt or soil for earth, a feather or incense for air, a candle or an image of a flame for fire, and a bowl of water or a seashell for water.

In addition to representing the elements, consider incorporating other natural elements into your indoor sacred space. Potted plants, for example, can bring vibrant, living energy into the space and help to maintain a connection to the earth. Choose plants that hold personal significance to you, whether for their aesthetic appeal, their magical properties, or their associations with your spiritual path. You might also include crystals, stones, or driftwood, which can carry the energy of the earth and its elemental forces.

Creating an altar within your indoor sacred space provides a focal point for your spiritual practice and a place to honor your beliefs and intentions. Your altar can be as simple or as elaborate as you wish, reflecting your unique spiritual path and personal aesthetic. Include sacred objects, symbols, and artwork that hold meaning for you and resonate with your practice, and arrange them in a manner that feels harmonious and balanced.

Finally, consider incorporating sensory elements into your indoor sacred space to create a fully immersive experience. Soft lighting, calming music or nature sounds, and the use of essential oils or incense can help to create an atmosphere of peace and serenity, allowing you to fully engage with your spiritual practice.

As for my own indoor sacred space, I have a large living room with a big bay window that is the size of a whole wall allowing for a lot of natural lighting. I created a room dedicated to meditation and spiritual practice. I also write in this room. I started by cleansing the space with sage and setting my intentions for peace and relaxation. I then chose a variety of indoor plants to bring life and vitality to the space. I also created several homemade terrariums and biomes using moss, rocks, and air plants.

To add color and texture, I hung a mandala tapestry on the wall and placed a few of my favorite crystals and stones on a small shelf. I also included a few books on mindfulness and spirituality to read during meditation.

Since creating my indoor sacred space, I've found that it's become a refuge from the chaos of everyday life. I start each morning with a meditation session in my sacred space and take breaks throughout the day to reconnect with my intentions. The plants and biomes require regular care, which has become a meditative practice in itself.

Cleansing and Charging Crystals

Cleansing and charging crystals are essential practices to ensure that they maintain their energetic purity and potency. Over time, crystals can absorb or store unwanted energies, which may hinder their effectiveness in your magical and spiritual work. By regularly cleansing and charging your crystals, you can restore their natural vibrational frequencies, enabling them to better support you in your witchcraft practice.

Cleansing a crystal removes any negative or stagnant energies it may have absorbed. There are several methods for cleansing crystals, each with its own benefits and considerations. One popular method is smudging, which involves using the smoke of sacred herbs like sage, cedar, or palo santo to purify the crystal. Gently pass the crystal through the smoke, allowing it to cleanse and neutralize any unwanted energies.

Another effective method for cleansing crystals is to bury them in the earth for a period of time, usually overnight or for 24 hours. The earth's natural energies work to absorb and neutralize any negativity within the crystal. After the allotted time, carefully dig up the crystal, and rinse it with clean water to remove any remaining dirt.

Water is another powerful cleansing agent, and some crystals can be cleansed by holding them under running water or placing them in a bowl of natural spring water or saltwater. Be mindful that some crystals, such as selenite or malachite, are water-sensitive and can be damaged by water. Always research your specific crystal before using this method.

Charging your crystals restores and enhances their energetic properties, allowing them to better serve your intentions. One common method for charging crystals is to place them under the light of the full moon. The moon's energy is said to amplify the crystal's natural vibrations, imbuing it with the lunar energy essential for many witchcraft practices. Simply place your crystals on a windowsill or outside in a safe space where they can absorb the moon's light.

Sunlight is another powerful source of energy for charging crystals. However, be cautious when using sunlight, as prolonged exposure to direct sunlight can cause some crystals, like amethyst or rose quartz, to fade. To charge your crystals with sunlight, place them outside or on a windowsill for a few hours during the early morning or late afternoon when the sunlight is less intense.

Crystal clusters or charging plates made of selenite or quartz can also be used to charge your crystals. These materials naturally amplify and transmit energy, making them ideal for recharging other crystals. Simply place your crystals on the cluster or charging plate for several hours or overnight to restore their energy.

Circle Casting

Creating a circle, or circle casting, is an essential practice in many forms of witchcraft, particularly in nature-based traditions like Green Witchcraft. The purpose of casting a circle is to create a sacred space within which to perform rituals, spells, and other magical workings. This sacred space is considered a safe and energetically charged environment that allows practitioners to focus their intentions and connect with the energies of the Earth and the elements.

To begin casting a circle, it is important to choose a suitable location. Ideally, this should be a quiet, undisturbed place where you can connect with the energies of the Earth and the elements. This may be indoors or outdoors, depending on your preference and available space. Before beginning the circle casting, make sure to cleanse the area of any negative energies or distractions. This can be done using various methods, such as smudging with sage or other herbs, sprinkling salt, or using a besom (a traditional broom made of natural materials) to symbolically sweep away any negative energy.

Once the area is cleansed, you can begin the process of casting the circle. Some practitioners prefer to use a tool, such as an athame (a ritual knife) or a wand, to physically trace the circle's perimeter, while others may simply use their index finger or the power of visualization. As you trace the circle, envision a protective barrier of energy being formed, which will serve to contain the energies raised during your magical workings and keep out any unwanted influences.

After the circle's perimeter has been established, it is customary to call upon the four elements – earth, air, fire, and water – and their corresponding cardinal directions – north, east, south, and west – to help protect and empower the circle. This can be done by invoking the elements and their associated spirits or deities, often accompanied by the use of symbolic tools or objects, such as candles, crystals, or representations of the elements.

Once the elements have been called upon, some practitioners may also choose to invite their personal deities, ancestors, or other spiritual guides to join them within the circle. This is often done through prayer, invocation, or a simple invitation spoken aloud.

With the circle cast and the energies of the elements and any invited spiritual beings present, you can now proceed with your magical workings, confident that you are working within a safe and sacred space. When your ritual or spell is complete, it is important to properly close the circle by thanking the elements and any spiritual beings for their assistance and releasing them from the circle. This can be done by reversing the process used to call upon them, moving counterclockwise around the circle and acknowledging each element and spiritual being in turn.

Finally, to fully close the circle, trace the perimeter once more, either physically or through visualization, and envision the protective barrier of energy dissipating. This signals the end of the ritual and allows the energies raised during the magical working to disperse or be channeled toward their intended purpose.

Green Energy

Green energy, also referred to as life energy, in the context of nature-based magic and ritual, refers to the vital life force that flows through the natural world, connecting all living beings and promoting growth, healing, and balance. This energy is harnessed and channeled by practitioners to empower their spiritual work and to deepen their connection with the earth and its cycles. Embracing green energy in one's practice enables a practitioner to tap into the wisdom and transformative power of nature, fostering a more harmonious and sustainable way of living and interacting with the environment.

One way to access green energy is through the practice of grounding, which involves connecting with the earth's energy to establish a strong foundation for one's spiritual work. This can be achieved through various techniques, such as walking barefoot on the earth, sitting or lying down on the ground, or visualizing roots extending from one's body into the soil. By grounding oneself, a practitioner not only attunes to the earth's energy but also releases any excess or stagnant energy, promoting balance and clarity in their spiritual practice.

Another approach to working with green energy is by incorporating the elements—earth, air, fire, and water—into one's rituals and spells. Each element carries its unique energetic signature, and by understanding and harnessing their properties, a green witch can enhance the potency of their magical work. For example, earth energy can be used for grounding and stability, air energy for communication and clarity, fire energy for transformation and action, and water energy for emotional healing and intuition. Practitioners may choose to represent the elements symbolically through the use of elemental tools, such as crystals, candles, incense, and water, or by working directly with natural elements like soil, wind, flames, and rain.

Green energy can also be accessed through working with plants, trees, and herbs in one's magical practice. Each plant possesses its unique energetic properties, which can be harnessed for healing, protection, manifestation, and more. By cultivating a garden, gathering wild plants, or simply connecting with the plant spirits through meditation and visualization, a green witch can deepen their understanding of the green world and its energetic offerings. Moreover, using ethically harvested plant materials in rituals, spells, and as offerings can strengthen the practitioner's bond with the earth and help to maintain a respectful, reciprocal relationship with the natural world.

Additionally, green energy can be found in the cycles and rhythms of the natural world, such as the changing seasons, the phases of the moon, and the daily cycle of the sun. By aligning one's spiritual practice with these natural cycles, a green witch can tap into the ebb and flow of energy, harnessing the unique qualities and opportunities each phase presents. Celebrating seasonal festivals, performing lunar rituals, and acknowledging solar transitions are just a few ways to attune oneself to the ever-changing energies of the earth and cosmos.

Herbal Magic

Herbal magic has been practiced for centuries as a way to harness the power of nature and the plant kingdom to support healing, transformation, and spiritual growth. From ancient civilizations to modern practitioners, people have used herbs for everything from medicinal purposes to spell-casting and ritual work.

At its core, herbal magic is about tapping into the inherent wisdom and energy of plants to support our own healing and growth. This might involve working with specific herbs for their medicinal properties, using herbs in spell-casting and ritual work, or simply cultivating a deeper connection to the natural world through the study and use of herbs.

One of the most important aspects of practicing herbal magic is developing a strong understanding of the properties and energies of different herbs. This might involve studying the medicinal properties of specific plants, learning about the symbolic meanings of different herbs in different cultures and traditions, or experimenting with different herbs to see how they affect your own energy and mood.

Another key aspect of herbal magic is learning to work with intention and focus. Whether you're using herbs to support physical healing or to enhance your meditation or ritual work, setting clear intentions and focusing your energy and attention on the desired outcome is essential.

It's important to approach herbal magic with a spirit of respect and reverence for the natural world. This might involve growing your own herbs, sourcing herbs sustainably from ethical sources, or offering gratitude and thanks to the plants themselves for their support and healing energy.

Ultimately, herbal magic is a deeply personal and individual practice that can be adapted and customized to fit your own unique needs and goals. Whether you're using herbs for physical healing, spiritual growth, or simply to connect more deeply with the natural world, incorporating herbal magic into your daily life can be a powerful way to support your own well-being and connection to the world around you.

Preparing Your Herbs

Preparing herbs is an important step in utilizing their full potential for medicinal or magical purposes. While there are different methods of preparation depending on the intended use of the herbs, there are some general guidelines that can be followed.

The first step is to source high-quality herbs from reputable suppliers. Whether you grow your own herbs or purchase them, it's important to ensure that they are free from pesticides, chemicals, and other contaminants that can diminish their potency or increase their toxicity.

Next, it's important to determine the best method of preparation for your intended use. This might involve making a tea or an infusion, creating a tincture or extract, or incorporating the herbs into a salve or oil.

For making teas or infusions, start by crushing or chopping the herbs into small pieces to release their oils and compounds. Then, bring water to a boil and pour it over the herbs, steeping for the recommended amount of time depending on the herb and its intended use.

For tinctures or extracts, the herbs are typically soaked in alcohol or vinegar for several weeks to extract their medicinal properties. It's important to use high-proof alcohol or vinegar to ensure that the extraction process is effective.

When creating a salve or oil, the herbs are typically infused into a carrier oil, such as olive or coconut oil, over a low heat for several hours. The resulting oil can be used topically for a variety of purposes.

It's important to store herbs properly to maintain their potency and effectiveness. Keep dried herbs in a cool, dry place away from direct sunlight, and store fresh herbs in the refrigerator in a sealed container.

In conclusion, preparing herbs is an important step in utilizing their full potential for medicinal or magical purposes. By sourcing high-quality herbs, determining the best method of preparation, and storing herbs properly, you can ensure that you are getting the most out of these powerful and transformative plants. Whether you are making a tea, creating a tincture, or infusing herbs into a salve or oil, taking the time to prepare your herbs with care and intention can enhance their healing and magical properties.

Extracting Herbal Energy

Extracting herbal energy is a process by which the energy and essence of plants are harnessed for spiritual and magical purposes. This process can involve various methods, such as creating an herbal infusion, making a tincture, or using essential oils.

To extract energy from herbs through infusion, start by crushing or chopping the herbs into small pieces to release their oils and compounds. Then, bring water to a boil and pour it over the herbs, steeping for the recommended amount of time depending on the herb and its intended use. As the herbs steep, their energy and essence are infused into the water, creating a powerful elixir.

Tinctures are another way to extract the energy of herbs. Tinctures involve soaking the herbs in alcohol or vinegar for several weeks to extract their medicinal properties. During this process, the energy and essence of the herbs are infused into the liquid, creating a potent and concentrated extract.

Essential oils are another powerful way to extract the energy of herbs. Essential oils are created by distilling or extracting the volatile compounds from plants, which are then concentrated into a potent oil. These oils can be used in aromatherapy, applied topically, or ingested for their healing and magical properties.

It's important to approach the process of extracting herbal energy with intention and respect for the plants. Before extracting energy from any plant, take the time to research its properties and uses, and make sure to source high-quality herbs from reputable suppliers.

In conclusion, extracting herbal energy is a powerful way to harness the magical and healing properties of plants. Whether through infusions, tinctures, or essential oils, taking the time to extract the energy and essence of plants can enhance your spiritual and magical practices. Remember to approach the process with intention and respect, and always research the properties and uses of each herb before use. With these practices in mind, you can tap into the transformative power of herbs and create a deeper connection with the natural world.

Blessing Your Creations

When working with herbs, it's important to honor their energy and essence by blessing them before use. This can be done in many ways, depending on your personal beliefs and practices. Here are a few suggestions for blessing your herbal creations:

Set an intention: Before working with your herbs, take a moment to set an intention for their use. This can be as simple as stating your intention out loud or silently in your mind. By setting an intention, you are directing your energy and focus towards your desired outcome.

Call upon the elements: Many practitioners of herbal magic believe in the power of the elements - earth, air, fire, water, and spirit - to enhance the energy of their herbs. You can invoke the elements by lighting a candle, burning incense, sprinkling water or salt, or simply calling upon their energy.

Use prayer or visualization: You can also bless your herbs through prayer or visualization. This can involve speaking a blessing or prayer over your herbs, visualizing their energy being infused with light and love, or simply holding them in your hands and sending positive energy towards them.

Use symbols or talismans: Some people like to use symbols or talismans to bless their herbs, such as placing them on a specific altar or using a particular crystal or piece of jewelry. You can also create your own symbol or talisman to use in your herbal work.

Thank the plants: Finally, it's important to remember to thank the plants themselves for their gifts. You can do this by offering a prayer of gratitude or simply taking a moment to acknowledge the energy and essence of the plant.

Blessing your herbal creations is a simple but powerful way to honor the energy and essence of the plants you work with. By setting an intention, calling upon the elements, using prayer or visualization, using symbols or talismans, and thanking the plants, you can enhance the magic and healing properties of your herbs and create a deeper connection with the natural world.

Growing Houseplants

Incorporating plants throughout your home can have a profound impact on both your physical and emotional well-being, as well as your connection to nature. By integrating greenery into your living spaces, you can transform your home into a sanctuary that nurtures and supports your spiritual practice while providing numerous practical benefits.

One of the most significant advantages of having plants in the house is the improvement of indoor air quality. Plants act as natural air purifiers, absorbing harmful pollutants and toxins while releasing oxygen through the process of photosynthesis. This can lead to cleaner, fresher air, reducing the risk of respiratory issues and promoting overall well-being. Some plants, such as spider plants, snake plants, and peace lilies, are particularly effective at removing common indoor air pollutants.

In addition to purifying the air, plants can also help regulate humidity levels within the home. Through the process of transpiration, plants release moisture into the air, helping to maintain a comfortable and balanced indoor environment. This can be especially beneficial during winter months when indoor air tends to become dry and stagnant, potentially leading to respiratory issues and dry skin.

The presence of plants in the home can also have a positive impact on mental health and well-being. Numerous studies have shown that being in the presence of plants can reduce stress levels, increase feelings of relaxation, and promote a sense of calm and serenity. By bringing the soothing energy of nature into your living space, you can create a more harmonious and peaceful environment that supports emotional balance and resilience.

Beyond their physical and emotional benefits, incorporating plants throughout your home can also serve as a powerful reminder of your connection to the natural world. For practitioners of green magic and nature-based spirituality, the presence of living, growing plants can help reinforce the belief in the interconnectedness of all living beings and the sacredness of the earth. By caring for and nurturing plants, you are actively engaging in a relationship with the natural world, fostering a deeper sense of connection and reverence for the earth.

Selecting plants with specific magical or spiritual properties can further enhance the benefits of having plants in the house. For example, you might choose plants that are associated with protection, such as rosemary or sage, to create a sense of safety and security within your home. Alternatively, plants like lavender or chamomile can be chosen for their calming and soothing properties, promoting a peaceful atmosphere.

When incorporating plants into your home, consider the specific needs and preferences of each plant, ensuring that they have access to the appropriate levels of light, water, and nutrients. By tending to the needs of your plants, you are not only supporting their growth and vitality, but also actively engaging in the practice of nurturing and caring for the earth, fostering a deeper connection to the natural world and its cycles.

Grounding and Earthing

Grounding, sometimes also referred to as earthing, is a powerful technique that helps us to connect with the Earth's energy and reestablish our balance and harmony. By practicing grounding, we can release any negative energy, tension, or stress that we might be carrying within us, and in turn, absorb the Earth's positive, stabilizing energy. This can lead to a greater sense of well-being, both physically and emotionally, and help us feel more connected to the natural world.

One popular method of grounding is walking barefoot outside on grass, sand, or soil. This direct contact with the Earth's surface allows our bodies to absorb its natural energy, which can help to neutralize any negative energy we may be carrying. As we walk, we can focus on the sensations beneath our feet and the rhythm of our breath, which can help to quiet our minds and bring us into the present moment.

Another grounding technique is the visualization of roots extending from the base of our spine or our feet and connecting with the Earth. By envisioning these roots burrowing deep into the ground, we can imagine the flow of energy between our bodies and the Earth. This can help to anchor us and create a sense of stability and balance.

Meditation is yet another powerful grounding method. By sitting or standing on the Earth's surface and focusing on our breath or the sensations in our bodies, we can become more attuned to the Earth's energy and our connection to it. This can lead to a deeper sense of peace and well-being.

Practicing yoga or other forms of movement outdoors can also help to ground us, as we are able to physically connect with the Earth while engaging in activities that promote mindfulness and presence. The combination of the physical movement and the connection to the Earth can create a powerful and grounding experience.

Incorporating grounding practices into our daily lives can have a significant impact on our overall well-being. By taking the time to consciously connect with the Earth and its energy, we can foster a greater sense of balance and harmony within ourselves and strengthen our bond with the natural world.

My Fairy Garden

When we first moved into our home, the backyard was little more than a hillside leading up to the woods with overgrown grass, weeds, and wild entangled muscadine vines. But I knew I wanted to create a space that felt like a life-size fairy garden, surrounded by all kinds of wildlife and birds.

I started by sketching out a rough plan for the space, mapping out where I wanted to place natural stairs and paths made with stones and moss. I also wanted to terraform the hillside to create a multi-level space for planting vegetables, fruits, and herbs.

The first step was to clear away the debris and overgrowth, so we cut down vines, raked leaves, cut down some small trees, and broke up the soil. We then laid out large stones to create steps and paths and filled in the gaps with moss and smaller stones.

To create the multi-level garden, we built up the hillside with topsoil and created raised beds using natural stone walls. We planted a variety of vegetables and herbs, including tomatoes, peppers, basil, and lavender.

Next, we turned our attention to the pond. We dug out a shallow depression and lined it with a rubber pond liner. We added a small waterfall and surrounded the pond with natural stones and plants. Within days, the pond was teeming with life, attracting frogs, dragonflies, and all cardinals, bluebirds, and finches.

To personalize the space, we added a small cherub birdfeeder statue that I thrifted and hung wind chimes from the trees. We also found a few more smaller garden statues like mushrooms and turtles. We then added a small table and chairs for quiet reflection and meditation. We made an entrance trellis and planted vining roses. We also plan to add a garden gazebo to the space eventually.

As the weeks went by, our outdoor sacred space began to take shape. Birds and butterflies flitted among the flowers, and I often spotted squirrels, rabbits, and deer grazing in the nearby woods. I found myself spending more and more time in the garden, cultivating a sense of peace and tranquility that I carried with me throughout the day. I would love to expand my outdoor sacred space to be like the Secret Garden one day and each day that I get to work on my garden is a spiritual experience that is grounding and rewarding and will be for years to come, for my children and theirs.

Ritual Examples

Rituals can take various forms, from simple daily practices such as lighting a candle to more elaborate ceremonies involving the casting of circles, invocation of deities, and the use of various magical tools and symbols. In the following section I will provide several examples of rituals that can be incorporated into your witchcraft practice. It is essential to remember that witchcraft is a highly personal and adaptable spiritual path, and you are encouraged to modify these rituals to fit your own beliefs, preferences, and needs. Trust your intuition and be guided by your connection to the natural world, the elements, and the energy that flows within and around you. Your rituals should reflect your unique spiritual journey, and by personalizing them, you can create a practice that truly resonates with your soul.

Ritual to Honor the Earth

This ritual is designed to help you connect with the Earth and express gratitude for its abundant gifts. By performing this ritual, you will deepen your bond with nature and strengthen your green witchcraft practice.

Ritual Items:

A small bowl of water (preferably rainwater or water from a natural source)

A green or brown candle

A small dish of soil or sand

A small dish of salt

An offering of flowers, leaves, or herbs (preferably collected from your local area)

A small flat stone or crystal (such as quartz, jasper, or agate)

Begin by choosing a quiet, comfortable location outdoors where you feel a strong connection to nature. Ideally, this should be a place that is surrounded by plants, trees, or other natural elements. Set up a small altar or space to perform your ritual by arranging the ritual items in a way that feels meaningful to you. Place the bowl of water, dish of soil, dish of salt, and the candle in the center.

Once your space is prepared, light the green or brown candle, and take a moment to ground yourself. Close your eyes and take a few deep breaths, focusing on the sensation of the earth beneath your feet and the air around you.

Next, hold the small flat stone or crystal in your hands and state your intention for the ritual. You may say something like, "I am here to honor and connect with the Earth and to express my gratitude for its gifts." Feel the energy of the Earth flowing through the stone or crystal and visualize it grounding and balancing you.

Now, take the bowl of water and gently pour it over the dish of soil or sand, symbolizing the union of water and earth. As you do this, say a few words of gratitude for the nourishment and sustenance the Earth provides, such as, "I thank you, Earth, for the food, shelter, and beauty you offer."

Sprinkle the salt over the soil and water mixture, representing the purifying and protective qualities of the Earth. As you do so, express your gratitude for the Earth's ability to cleanse and heal, saying something like, "I thank you, Earth, for your cleansing and healing energy that protects and nurtures us."

Place the offering of flowers, leaves, or herbs on the soil and water mixture. As you do this, say a few words of appreciation for the Earth's endless cycle of growth and renewal, such as, "I thank you, Earth, for your ever-present cycle of growth, transformation, and renewal."

To complete the ritual, take a few moments to meditate on your connection to the Earth and the gratitude you feel. When you are ready, snuff out the candle, and leave the space, knowing that you have honored the Earth and deepened your connection to nature.

Blessing of Tranquil Waters

This ritual is designed to invoke feelings of peace and tranquility, as well as to promote emotional healing and balance. By connecting with the calming energy of water, you can cultivate a serene and harmonious atmosphere in your life and your magical practice.

Ritual Items:

A small bowl of water (preferably collected from a natural source such as a river, lake, or ocean)

A white or light blue candle

A small dish of sea salt or Himalayan salt

A piece of clear quartz, amethyst, or other calming crystal

A small driftwood or wooden wand (optional)

A few drops of lavender or chamomile essential oil (optional)

Begin by choosing a quiet and comfortable location near a body of water, if possible. This could be a beach, a riverbank, or a lake shore. If you don't have access to a natural body of water, you can perform this ritual indoors near a water feature or in a quiet space where you feel calm and at ease. Set up a small altar or space to perform your ritual by arranging the ritual items in a way that feels meaningful to you. Place the bowl of water, the candle, the dish of salt, and the crystal in the center.

Once your space is prepared, light the white or light blue candle, and take a moment to ground yourself. Close your eyes and take a few deep breaths, focusing on the sensation of the water around you and the air on your skin.

Hold the calming crystal in your hands and state your intention for the ritual. You may say something like, "I am here to invoke the tranquil and healing energy of water to bring peace and balance into my life and my practice." Visualize the soothing energy of water flowing through the crystal and into your body, calming your mind and emotions.

Next, take the bowl of water and gently pour it over the dish of salt, symbolizing the purifying and calming properties of water and salt. As you do this, say a few words of gratitude for the healing and soothing powers of water, such as, "I thank the tranquil waters for their ability to cleanse, heal, and restore balance to my mind, body, and spirit."

If you choose to use essential oil, add a few drops to the bowl of water and salt mixture. As you do this, say a few words of appreciation for the added calming energy of the chosen oil, such as, "I thank the calming essence of lavender (or chamomile) for its soothing and peaceful energy that enhances this blessing."

With the driftwood or wooden wand (or your fingers, if you prefer), gently stir the water and salt mixture, infusing it with your intention for tranquility and emotional healing. Visualize the water absorbing your intention and becoming a powerful tool for peace and balance.

To complete the ritual, take a few moments to meditate on the calming energy of the water and the blessings it brings. When you are ready, snuff out the candle, and return the blessed water to the natural body of water or pour it on the earth to disperse its energy. Leave the space with a sense of serenity, knowing that you have connected with the tranquil energy of water and created a peaceful atmosphere in your life and practice.

Herbal Incense of Protection

This ritual involves creating and burning a protective herbal incense blend to surround a person or space with a barrier of safety and positive energy. By focusing your intentions on the person or space you wish to protect, the incense's magical properties will help to ward off negativity and maintain a secure and harmonious environment.

Ritual Items:

A fireproof dish or cauldron

A blend of protective herbs (such as rosemary, sage, lavender, and cedar)

A lighter or matches

A small feather or fan (optional)

A white or black candle

A picture, personal item, or written name of the person you wish to protect (optional)

Begin by preparing your ritual space in a quiet and comfortable location, either indoors or outdoors. Set up a small altar or area to perform the ritual by arranging the ritual items in a way that feels meaningful to you. Place the fireproof dish or cauldron, herbal blend, and candle in the center.

Light the white or black candle, symbolizing protection and the guiding light that keeps the person or space safe. Take a moment to ground yourself, close your eyes, and take a few deep breaths, focusing on your intention to protect the person or space.

If you have a picture, personal item, or written name of the person you wish to protect, place it near the candle. Take a moment to visualize this person surrounded by a shield of protective energy and state your intention for the ritual. You may say something like, "I call upon the protective powers of these sacred herbs to surround [person's name] with a barrier of safety, love, and positive energy."

Place a small amount of the protective herbal blend into the fireproof dish or cauldron. Light the herbs using the lighter or matches, allowing them to smolder and release their fragrant smoke. As the incense burns, visualize the protective energy of the herbs enveloping the person or space you wish to protect, creating a barrier against negativity and harm.

If you have a small feather or fan, you may use it to gently waft the smoke in the direction of the person or space you wish to protect. As you do this, say a few words to reinforce your intention, such as, "With this protective incense, I surround [person's name or space] with a shield of safety, love, and positive energy."

Allow the incense to burn out completely and take a moment to reflect on the protection you have provided. When you feel the ritual is complete, extinguish the candle and thank the protective energies of the herbs for their assistance.

Invocation of Gaia

This ritual is designed to invoke the spirit and energy of Gaia, the Earth Goddess and Mother of all life. By connecting with Gaia's nurturing and grounding energy, you can tap into her wisdom, strength, and healing abilities. The invocation used in this ritual is a poetic tribute to Gaia, celebrating her life-giving essence and expressing gratitude for her presence.

Ritual Items:

A green, brown, or white candle

A representation of Gaia (a statue, picture, or natural item such as a stone or plant)

A bowl of soil or a potted plant

Incense or essential oil with earthy scents (such as patchouli, sandalwood, or cedar)

A quiet and comfortable space in which to perform the ritual

Instructions:

Begin by preparing your ritual space. Choose a quiet and comfortable location, either indoors or outdoors. Set up a small altar or area to perform the ritual by arranging the ritual items in a way that feels meaningful to you. Place the candle, representation of Gaia, bowl of soil or potted plant, and incense or essential oil at the center.

Light the candle, symbolizing the life-giving warmth and energy of Gaia. Burn the incense or diffuse the essential oil to create an earthy atmosphere that connects you to the essence of Gaia.

Sit or stand comfortably in front of your altar and take a few deep breaths to ground yourself. Close your eyes and visualize the energy of the Earth beneath you, feeling its strength and stability.

When you feel connected to the Earth, recite the following invocation:

"Gaia, Mother of all life,
Beneath your nurturing embrace,
We find solace and strength,
In your eternal grace.

From the depths of your core,
To the reaches of your skies,
Your wisdom and love,
In every breath, we recognize.

With gratitude, we call upon you,
As we seek your guidance and might,

Embrace us in your loving arms,
And illuminate our path with light.

Oh, Gaia, our Earth Mother divine,
We honor you now and for all time."

Take a moment to meditate on the energy of Gaia, feeling her presence and power within you and all around you. If you have a specific intention or request, take this time to communicate it silently or verbally to Gaia, knowing that she hears and understands your needs.

When you feel your connection to Gaia has been established and your intention has been heard, thank her for her presence and guidance. Extinguish the candle and allow the incense to burn out.

After the ritual, spend some time in nature, tending to a garden, or caring for a plant to strengthen your connection to Gaia and honor her life-giving essence.

Garden of Abundance

This ritual is designed to bless your garden with vigorous growth, abundance, and harmony. By incorporating the elements and the power of a bell, you create a sacred space that invites the natural energies to promote the flourishing of your garden.

Ritual Items:

A bell or chime

A small bowl of water (representing the element of water)

A feather or incense (representing the element of air)

A bowl of soil (representing the element of earth)

A small dish of salt (representing the element of fire, as salt is born of fire)

Your garden or a container garden, if space is limited

Instructions:

Begin by preparing your ritual space. Go to your garden, whether it's an outdoor space or a container garden inside. Ensure the area is clean and free from clutter to create a harmonious environment for the ritual.

Start by placing the four elemental representations around your garden or container. The bowl of water represents the water element, essential for the growth and nourishment of the plants. The feather or incense represents the air element, providing the plants with the necessary carbon dioxide and oxygen. The bowl of soil represents the earth element, the foundation and support for the plants. The dish of salt represents the fire element, symbolizing the warmth and energy required for growth.

Once you have placed the elemental representations, stand in the center of your garden or near your container garden. Close your eyes and take a few deep breaths, connecting yourself with the energies of the earth and the life that surrounds you.

When you feel grounded and connected, open your eyes and take the bell or chime in your hand. Begin to walk around your garden, ringing the bell or chime as you go. As you do this, say the following words:

"By the power of Earth, Air, Fire, and Water,
I call upon the spirits of abundance and growth,
To bless this garden with life and vigor,
With each ringing sound, may these energies flow."

As you continue to walk around your garden, visualize the sound of the bell or chime dispersing any stagnant or negative energies, creating a sacred space for your plants to grow and thrive.

When you have completed your walk around the garden, return to the center, and take a moment to feel the energy shift in your space. Visualize the plants in your garden growing strong, healthy, and abundant, filled with the blessings of the elements.

To close the ritual, say the following words:

"Thank you, spirits of abundance and growth,
For blessing this garden with your presence,
May this space be filled with harmony and life,
And may the blessings of the elements be ever bright."

Take a moment to express gratitude for the energies that have been called upon, and then carefully collect the elemental representations. You may choose to leave them in your garden as a reminder of the blessing, or you can return them to their original places.

Remember to care for your garden regularly, tending to its needs with love and intention.

Yggdrasil's Communion

This ritual is designed to help you commune with the forest spirits by meditating in front of a tree. The gentle sound of a bell initiates and concludes the communion, creating a sacred space for you to connect with the energies of the natural world.

Ritual Items:

A bell or chime
A tree in a forest or a natural area where you feel a connection with nature

Begin by finding a tree within a forest or natural area that you feel drawn to. This tree will serve as your anchor during the meditation and the connection point with the forest spirits. Ensure the area surrounding the tree is clean and free from clutter to create a harmonious environment for the ritual.

Stand in front of the tree, holding the bell or chime in your hand. Close your eyes and take a few deep breaths, grounding yourself and connecting with the energies of the tree and the forest.

When you feel grounded and connected, open your eyes, and gently ring the bell or chime three times to initiate the communion with the forest spirits. As the sound reverberates, say the following words:

"By the sound of this bell, I invite the spirits of the forest,
To share with me your wisdom and presence,
In this sacred space, I open my heart and mind,
To listen, learn, and commune with your essence."

After reciting these words, sit comfortably at the base of the tree. Close your eyes and begin to meditate, focusing on your breath and allowing your awareness to expand into the surrounding environment. Feel the energy of the tree and the forest spirits and open yourself to any messages or insights that they may share with you.

Take as much time as needed in meditation, allowing the connection with the forest spirits to grow and deepen. When you feel that the communion is complete, gently ring the bell or chime three times once again to signal the end of the meditation and to thank the forest spirits for their presence.

To close the ritual, say the following words:

"Thank you, spirits of the forest, for your wisdom and connection,
May the bond we have forged today grow and strengthen,
114

As I walk through these woods, may our hearts intertwine,
With gratitude and love, I honor this sacred time."

Take a moment to express gratitude for the energies that have been called upon, and then slowly rise from your seated position. As you leave the area, remember to take with you the insights and connections made during the communion, carrying them with you as a reminder of the sacred bond between you and the forest spirits.

Growing a Garden

Even without access to suitable ground, you can still reap the benefits of gardening by growing plants in containers. Container gardening is a versatile and adaptable approach that can be tailored to fit any space, no matter how small. A simple kitchen window garden, for example, can serve as a powerful means of connecting with nature and experiencing the joys of nurturing plant life. By cultivating herbs, flowers, or even small vegetables in pots or other containers placed on a windowsill or balcony, you can enjoy the pleasures of gardening and the satisfaction of growing your own ingredients for rituals and meals. This small-scale approach to gardening can help you develop a more intimate connection with the plants you grow, as you tend to their needs and witness their growth up close. Additionally, a kitchen window garden can serve as a daily reminder of your connection to the natural world, infusing your home with the vibrant energy of living plants and fostering a deeper appreciation for the Earth and its many gifts.

Designing Your Garden

Creating a garden is one of the best ways to cultivate a deeper connection with nature and enhance one's spiritual practice. The process of setting up a garden involves careful consideration of both practical and spiritual aspects, ensuring that the space is functional and reflective of the individual's unique spiritual beliefs and intentions.

When designing a spiritual garden, one must first select a location that resonates with their spiritual energy and provides a sense of tranquility. This space should be a sanctuary, offering privacy and a refuge from the outside world. It's essential to consider factors such as sunlight, soil quality, and accessibility when choosing the perfect spot. Ideally, the location should receive ample sunlight and have fertile, well-draining soil to support plant growth. Furthermore, the garden should be easily accessible, allowing the individual to visit and tend to it regularly.

Next, consider the layout and design of the spiritual garden. The design should reflect the individual's personal tastes and preferences, as well as their spiritual beliefs and intentions. Some may opt for a traditional or symmetrical design, while others might prefer a more organic, free-flowing arrangement. Incorporating elements such as pathways, seating areas, and focal points can help create a sense of structure and flow within the space, guiding visitors through the garden and inviting moments of contemplation and reflection.

When selecting plants for the spiritual garden, it's crucial to consider both their practical and symbolic attributes. Some individuals may choose plants based on their significance in their spiritual practice or their associations with specific deities or energies. For example, lavender can be used for its calming properties and association with spiritual purification, while rosemary is known for its protective and healing energies. Additionally, the garden may include plants that serve as sources of food or medicine, such as herbs, fruits, and vegetables. This aspect of the garden emphasizes the interconnectedness of nature and human well-being, encouraging a sense of gratitude and reverence for the Earth and its bounty.

Incorporating elements of sacred geometry, such as circles, spirals, or labyrinths, can enhance the spiritual potency of the garden. These shapes hold symbolic meaning in many spiritual traditions, and their presence in the garden can serve as a reminder of the individual's connection to the cosmos and the underlying patterns that govern the natural world. Including features like water fountains, bird feeders, or wind chimes can also enhance the sensory experience of the garden, providing opportunities for mindfulness and meditation.

Another thing to consider is the inclusion of sacred spaces or altars. These areas can be as simple or elaborate as desired, serving as focal points for ritual, meditation, or prayer. Altars can be dedicated to specific deities, ancestors, or spiritual forces and adorned with offerings, symbols, or objects that hold personal significance. These sacred spaces help to anchor the spiritual energy of the garden, creating a powerful atmosphere conducive to spiritual growth and healing.

Planting Tips

Here are some planting tips to consider for your garden, these are just basic introductory tips and you should research further before planting although to be honest, you'll likely learn the most from trial and error so don't be afraid to make mistakes!

Choose the right location: Select a spot that receives adequate sunlight and has well-draining soil. Consider the specific needs of the plants you wish to grow and their significance in your practice.

Create a sacred space: Dedicate a section of your garden for meditation, rituals, or offerings. This space can include an altar, statues, or other symbolic elements that resonate with your spiritual practice.

Start with healthy soil: Test your soil's pH and nutrient levels to ensure it provides the proper environment for your plants. Amend the soil with organic matter such as compost or aged manure to improve fertility and structure.

Plant according to the moon phases: In witchcraft, moon phases can play a significant role in gardening. You can plant during the waxing moon for growth and wait until the waning moon for pruning or harvesting. This can help enhance the plants' magical properties and harness lunar energy.

Use companion planting: Planting certain plants together can improve their growth, health, and yield. Research which plants have beneficial relationships and incorporate these combinations into your garden design.

Practice organic gardening: Avoid synthetic chemicals and opt for organic methods to control pests and diseases. This not only benefits the environment but also aligns with the principles of green witchcraft and nature worship.

Grow plants with magical properties: Choose plants that hold specific magical or spiritual significance, such as herbs for protection, healing, or love. These plants can be used in spells, rituals, or as offerings to deities.

Connect with plant spirits: As you tend your garden, take the time to communicate with the plants and develop a deeper relationship with their spirits. This can enhance your magical practice and foster a deeper connection with nature.

Mulch and conserve water: Apply a layer of organic mulch around plants to help retain moisture, suppress weeds, and regulate soil temperature. Use water-saving techniques such as drip irrigation, rain barrels, or watering during the cooler hours of the day.

Rotate crops: Practice crop rotation to prevent soil-borne diseases and pests and maintain soil fertility. This is especially important for growing vegetables and herbs in a sustainable manner.

Learn about the medicinal properties of plants: Grow plants with known medicinal properties and educate yourself on their uses. This can expand your herbal knowledge and enhance your green witchcraft practice.

Create a wildlife-friendly garden: Plant native species to provide food and shelter for local wildlife, such as birds, bees, and butterflies. This encourages biodiversity and supports the ecosystem, aligning with the principles of nature worship.

Harvest ethically: When collecting plant material for spells or rituals, take only what you need and always express gratitude for the plant's energy and sacrifice. This fosters a respectful relationship with the natural world.

Practice seed-saving: Save seeds from your plants to preserve their genetic diversity and to continue the cycle of growth and regeneration. This act honors the sacred cycles of life and death in nature.

Utilize garden waste for spellwork: Incorporate garden waste, such as dried leaves, flowers, or twigs, into your spells and rituals. This can help you harness the energy of the garden and create a deeper connection with your plants.

Meditate and perform rituals in the garden: Connect with nature and the energies of your plants by meditating, performing rituals, or casting spells in the garden. This can help you attune to the natural rhythms of the earth and strengthen your spiritual practice.

Caring for Your Garden Naturally

Maintaining a garden in a natural, ethical, and harm-free way requires a holistic approach that emphasizes sustainability, respect for nature, and responsible stewardship. One of the first steps in this process is to select plants that are well-suited to your local climate and soil conditions. By choosing native or well-adapted plants, you can minimize the need for resource-intensive inputs such as water, fertilizers, and pesticides, while also supporting local biodiversity and ecosystems.

Organic gardening methods are a cornerstone of ethical and harm-free garden maintenance. These methods prioritize the use of natural and eco-friendly alternatives to synthetic fertilizers, pesticides, and herbicides. Instead of relying on chemical treatments, organic gardeners can use compost, aged manure, and other organic materials to enrich their soil and provide essential nutrients for their plants. Beneficial insects and companion planting techniques can also be employed to control pests and diseases naturally, without resorting to harmful chemicals that can damage the environment and disrupt the balance of the ecosystem.

Water conservation is another important aspect of sustainable and ethical garden maintenance. By using water-efficient irrigation methods, such as drip irrigation or soaker hoses, gardeners can minimize water waste and reduce the impact of their gardening practices on local water resources. Collecting rainwater in barrels or other containers is another effective way to conserve water and lessen the environmental footprint of your garden.

In addition to these sustainable practices, ethical gardeners should also be mindful of the impact their actions have on local wildlife and the broader ecosystem. This includes taking steps to create a garden that is inviting and supportive of native pollinators, birds, and other beneficial creatures. Planting a diverse range of flowering plants that provide nectar and pollen throughout the growing season, as well as creating nesting sites and habitat for insects and birds, can help foster a vibrant and interconnected garden ecosystem.

Gardeners practicing harm-free maintenance should also be attentive to the ethical treatment of the plants themselves. This means harvesting plant materials responsibly and with gratitude, taking care not to overharvest or damage the plants in the process. It's essential to recognize the interconnectedness of all living beings and the role plants play in supporting the health and wellbeing of the entire ecosystem.

Composting is another way to maintain a garden in a natural and ethical manner. By recycling organic waste from your kitchen and garden, you can create a nutrient-rich, environmentally friendly soil amendment that reduces the need for synthetic fertilizers and supports healthy plant growth. Composting not only helps to close the loop of nutrient cycling in your garden but also reduces the amount of waste that ends up in landfills.

Create and Craft

Tinctures

Making a tincture is a simple process that allows you to harness the healing properties of plants and create a concentrated, easy-to-use herbal remedy. A tincture is a liquid extract made by soaking plant material in a solvent, typically alcohol, to draw out the active constituents of the plant. The following paragraphs detail the steps involved in creating a tincture, from selecting the appropriate plant material to storing and using the final product.

First and foremost, it is crucial to choose high-quality plant material for your tincture. You can either use fresh or dried herbs, but it is essential that the plants are free of pesticides, mold, and other contaminants. If possible, harvest herbs from your own garden or source them from a trusted supplier who can guarantee their purity and potency. Ensure that the plant material is properly cleaned and free of dirt, insects, and debris before beginning the tincture-making process.

Next, you will need to select an appropriate solvent for your tincture. Most herbal tinctures use alcohol as a solvent, as it is highly effective at extracting a wide range of plant constituents, including alkaloids, glycosides, and essential oils. The ideal alcohol concentration for a tincture is between 40% and 60%. High-proof grain alcohol or vodka is commonly used, but if you prefer a non-alcoholic option, you can use vegetable glycerin or apple cider vinegar as your solvent. However, keep in mind that these alternatives may not extract the plant constituents as effectively as alcohol.

Once you have chosen your plant material and solvent, you will need to prepare the herbs for extraction. If using fresh herbs, finely chop or grind them to increase the surface area for extraction. For dried herbs, ensure they are properly crushed or ground before proceeding. Measure your herbs by weight and your solvent by volume to ensure an accurate ratio. A general guideline for the herb-to-solvent ratio is 1:5 (one part herb to five parts solvent) for dried herbs and 1:2 for fresh herbs.

Place the prepared plant material in a clean glass jar, ensuring that there is enough space for the solvent to cover the herbs completely. Pour the solvent over the herbs, making sure that they are fully submerged. If using fresh herbs, you may need to press them down slightly to release any trapped air bubbles. Seal the jar tightly and label it with the name of the plant material, the solvent used, and the date of preparation.

Store the jar in a cool, dark place, such as a cupboard or pantry, for at least two weeks to allow the plant constituents to be extracted by the solvent. During this time, it is essential to shake the jar gently at least once a day to help the extraction process. After the designated extraction period has passed, strain the liquid through a fine mesh strainer or cheesecloth, pressing firmly on the plant material to extract as much liquid as possible.

Transfer the strained liquid to a clean, dark glass bottle or dropper bottle for storage. Be sure to label the bottle with the name of the tincture, the date of preparation, and any relevant information about the plant material and solvent used. Store the finished tincture in a cool, dark place, away from heat and sunlight. Properly stored tinctures can last several years.

When using your tincture, consult a reputable herbal reference or consult a qualified herbalist to determine the appropriate dosage for your specific needs. Generally, tinctures are administered in small doses, typically measured in drops, and can be taken directly under the tongue or diluted in water or another liquid. It is important to start with a low dose and gradually increase it as needed, paying close attention to your body's response and any potential side effects. Remember that herbal remedies can be potent, and it is essential to use them with caution and respect for their potential effects on your body.

Incorporating tinctures into your green magic practice can provide a powerful and convenient way to harness the healing properties of plants. Tinctures can be used for a variety of purposes, including supporting physical health, emotional wellbeing, and spiritual growth. As a practitioner of green magic, you may choose to create tinctures from plants that hold specific significance to your practice or align with your personal energetic needs.

126

As you become more experienced in making tinctures, you may wish to experiment with combining different herbs to create custom blends tailored to your unique needs and intentions. When crafting these blends, consider not only the individual properties of each plant but also how their energies may interact and complement one another.

Additionally, tinctures can be incorporated into your ritual work and sacred spaces. For example, you may use a tincture as an anointing oil to consecrate ritual tools or to bless and cleanse your sacred space. You can also use tinctures in meditation or visualization exercises, allowing the plant energies to support your spiritual journey and enhance your connection to the natural world.

The following is a list of herbs you could potentially use in your tinctures and what they are typically used for, once again I have to stress that you should always consult with a medical professional before trying any of these tinctures, especially if you're pregnant, nursing, or taking medications.

Echinacea: Boosts the immune system and fights infections, particularly during cold and flu season.

Peppermint: Alleviates digestive issues, headaches, nausea, and provides relief from cold and flu symptoms.

Chamomile: Promotes relaxation, reduces anxiety, and aids in sleep; also soothes digestive discomfort.

Valerian: Relieves anxiety, stress, and insomnia; acts as a natural sleep aid.

St. John's Wort: Helps alleviate mild to moderate depression and anxiety and supports emotional well-being.

Milk Thistle: Supports liver health and detoxification and helps protect the liver from damage.

Dandelion: Acts as a diuretic, supports liver health, and assists with detoxification.

Ginkgo Biloba: Improves cognitive function, memory, and concentration; also supports healthy blood flow.

Lemon Balm: Calms anxiety, relieves stress, and promotes relaxation; also has antiviral properties.

Passionflower: Reduces anxiety and stress, and aids in sleep; particularly useful for nervous restlessness.

Elderberry: Strengthens the immune system, fights colds and flu, and reduces inflammation.

Turmeric: Provides anti-inflammatory and antioxidant support and promotes overall well-being.

Licorice Root: Supports adrenal health, soothes digestive discomfort, and provides relief from cough and sore throat.

Ginger: Alleviates nausea, indigestion, and inflammation, and supports overall digestion.

Hawthorn: Supports heart health, promotes healthy blood pressure, and improves circulation.

Nettle: Provides relief from allergies, supports joint health, and promotes healthy urinary function.

Astragalus: Boosts the immune system, supports energy levels, and improves overall vitality.

Yarrow: Helps stop bleeding, reduces inflammation, and aids in healing wounds and skin irritations.

Calendula: Promotes wound healing, reduces inflammation, and soothes irritated skin.

Burdock: Supports healthy liver function, detoxification, and skin health; also acts as a diuretic.

Making Herbal Incense

Creating herbal incense can enhance the atmosphere of your sacred space, deepen your connection to the elements, and amplify the energies of your intentions. Herbal incense can be utilized in rituals, spells, or simply to create a calming and harmonious atmosphere in your home. The process of making your own herbal incense is an opportunity to combine your knowledge of herbs with your intuition and intention, resulting in a powerful and unique blend that is aligned with your specific purpose.

To begin making your herbal incense, you'll first need to select the herbs, resins, and other natural materials that will comprise your blend. When choosing ingredients, consider both their magical properties and their scent. Some popular ingredients for herbal incense include sage, lavender, rosemary, cedar, frankincense, and myrrh. Research the properties and correspondences of each ingredient, and ensure they align with your intentions. For example, lavender is known for its calming and soothing properties, while sage is often used for cleansing and purification.

Once you've chosen your ingredients, prepare them by either grinding them in a mortar and pestle or using a coffee grinder designated for this purpose. Grinding the ingredients will release their natural oils and fragrances, creating a stronger scent when burned. Keep in mind that some herbs and resins are harder to grind than others, so you may need to use a combination of methods to achieve the desired consistency.

After grinding your ingredients, it's time to blend them together. As you mix your herbs and resins, focus on your intentions for the incense and visualize the energies of each ingredient coming together to create a powerful and harmonious blend. You may choose to add a few drops of essential oils to further enhance the scent and magical properties of your incense. Be sure to mix thoroughly, ensuring that all the components are evenly distributed throughout the blend.

130

Once your incense is blended, you can choose to either burn it immediately or let it sit for a few days to allow the fragrances to meld together. To burn your incense, you'll need a heat-safe dish or burner and a charcoal disc specifically designed for burning incense. Light the charcoal disc and allow it to heat up until it's glowing red and covered in a layer of ash. Then, carefully place a small amount of your incense blend onto the charcoal disc, using a spoon or your fingers. As the incense burns, it will release its fragrance and energies, filling your space with its magical properties.

The following is a list of commonly used herbs and oils used to create herbal incenses and their magical properties.

Sage: Purification, cleansing, and protection. Often used to cleanse spaces and remove negative energy.

Lavender: Calming, peace, and love. Promotes relaxation and healing.

Rosemary: Protection, purification, and memory. Associated with mental clarity and focus.

Cedar: Grounding, protection, and prosperity. Attracts positive energy and repels negativity.

Frankincense: Purification, spiritual growth, and meditation. Enhances spiritual connection and awareness.

Myrrh: Protection, purification, and healing. Often used in meditation and rituals for spiritual transformation.

Sandalwood: Calming, grounding, and spiritual growth. Encourages inner peace and higher consciousness.

Cinnamon: Prosperity, love, and success. Stimulates creativity and attracts good fortune.

Jasmine: Love, sensuality, and spiritual connection. Associated with lunar energies and the divine feminine.

Lemongrass: Cleansing, purification, and mental clarity. Helps to release negativity and invite positive energy.

Peppermint: Healing, purification, and mental clarity. Stimulates creativity and communication.

Palo Santo: Cleansing, purification, and spiritual protection. Often used to dispel negative energy and invite positive vibes.

Patchouli: Grounding, prosperity, and attraction. Associated with earth energies and abundance.

Ylang Ylang: Love, sensuality, and relaxation. Encourages emotional balance and harmony.

Rose: Love, emotional healing, and beauty. Attracts love and encourages self-love and compassion.

Eucalyptus: Healing, protection, and purification. Promotes mental clarity and emotional balance.

Chamomile: Calming, peace, and healing. Encourages relaxation and emotional well-being.

Basil: Prosperity, protection, and love. Attracts wealth and positive energy.

Orange: Joy, success, and abundance. Encourages creativity and positivity.

Clove: Protection, prosperity, and love. Boosts courage and personal power.

Juniper: Purification, protection, and healing. Often used to dispel negative energy and invite positive forces.

Bergamot: Uplifting, joy, and prosperity. Encourages emotional balance and positive energy.

Pine: Cleansing, protection, and grounding. Connects with earth energies and promotes strength and resilience.

Thyme: Courage, protection, and healing. Enhances psychic abilities and spiritual connection.

Vetiver: Grounding, protection, and prosperity. Promotes emotional balance and inner strength.

Spell Bags

A spell bag, also known as a mojo bag, gris-gris, or charm bag, is a small pouch filled with various ingredients that hold specific energies and intentions, typically used for protection, prosperity, love, or other magical purposes. Creating a spell bag is a personal and intuitive process, allowing the practitioner to infuse their intentions and energy into the materials and ingredients they choose.

Selecting the bag itself is an essential step in creating a spell bag. Consider the color, material, and size of the bag, as these factors can influence the energies and symbolism of the spell. Colors have different correspondences; for example, green is often associated with prosperity and abundance, while red is linked to love and passion. Choose a fabric that resonates with you or holds a particular meaning, such as silk for luxury, cotton for purity, or leather for strength.

When choosing the ingredients for your spell bag, consider their magical properties and how they align with your intention. Herbs, crystals, charms, and other items can be used to create a powerful and personalized talisman. Research the properties of each ingredient and ensure they harmonize with your purpose. For example, rose quartz might be used for love, while citrine could be included for abundance and success. It's essential to cleanse and consecrate each item before placing it in the bag, ensuring that any negative energies are removed and the item is charged with your intention.

Personal items can also be included in the spell bag to strengthen the connection between the practitioner and the intended outcome. A lock of hair, a small photograph, or a piece of clothing can serve as a powerful link, anchoring the energy of the spell to the individual. When incorporating personal items, be mindful of privacy and consent, particularly when working on behalf of others.

Once you have selected your ingredients, carefully place them inside the bag while focusing on your intention. As you fill the bag, visualize the energy of each item merging and amplifying your purpose. Some practitioners may choose to recite a chant or incantation during this process to further empower the spell bag. Once all ingredients are inside, securely close the bag by tying a knot, sewing it shut, or using a drawstring.

After creating the spell bag, it's crucial to activate and charge it with energy. This can be done through various methods such as anointing it with oils, passing it through incense smoke, or placing it in the moonlight or sunlight. Hold the bag in your hands and visualize it being filled with powerful energy, resonating with your intention.

Finally, carry the spell bag with you, place it in a specific location, or incorporate it into a ritual, depending on your purpose. Regularly cleanse, charge, and reinforce your intentions to maintain the potency of your spell bag. Keep in mind that the spell bag's energy may eventually wane, so be prepared to create a new one when needed. Remember that the power of a spell bag lies in the intention, energy, and connection you establish with it, making it a valuable tool in your magical practice..

Broommaking

Creating a traditional broom, also known as a besom, for use in magical rituals is a meaningful and practical endeavor. The besom is often used for cleansing and purifying spaces, as well as for protection and other ritual purposes. Making your own broom allows you to infuse your intentions and energy into the tool, strengthening your connection to it and enhancing its magical properties.

The first step in making a traditional broom is selecting the materials. The handle is typically made from a sturdy and durable wood, such as ash, oak, or birch. Each wood has its own unique properties and correspondences, so consider your intentions and preferences when choosing. For the bristles, natural materials such as straw, heather, or twigs from trees like willow or birch are often used. As with the handle, the type of material you choose for the bristles will depend on your specific intentions and personal preferences.

Before beginning the construction process, it's important to cleanse and consecrate the materials. This can be done through various methods such as smudging with sage, sprinkling with saltwater, or passing through the smoke of an incense. Ensure that any negative energies are removed and that the materials are imbued with your intentions.

To create the broom handle, select a straight and sturdy branch or wooden dowel, and carefully remove any leaves, twigs, or rough bark. You may choose to sand the wood for a smoother finish or carve symbols, runes, or other designs into the handle to enhance its magical properties. Once the handle is prepared, set it aside.

Next, prepare the bristles by gathering the chosen material into a bundle. Ensure the bundle is thick and uniform, with the bristles aligned at one end. You may need to trim the bristles for a more even appearance. Measure the bundle against the handle to determine the desired length and trim if necessary.

Attach the bristles to the handle using a strong, natural cord or twine. Hemp, cotton, or jute are popular choices for their durability and eco-friendly properties. Begin by wrapping the cord tightly around the top of the bristle bundle, ensuring it is secure. Then, position the handle against the bristles and continue to wrap the cord around both the bristles and the handle, working your way down to create a firm and secure connection. Knot the cord and trim any excess.

Once the bristles are securely attached to the handle, take a moment to consecrate and bless your newly created besom. This can be done through a simple ritual or meditation, infusing the broom with your intentions and purpose. You may also choose to anoint it with oils or pass it through incense smoke to further empower the tool.

With your traditional broom now complete, you can use it in your magical rituals for cleansing, protection, and other purposes. Remember to care for your besom, regularly cleansing and recharging its energies to ensure its continued potency and effectiveness in your magical practice.

Balms

Balms are versatile and valuable tools in magical practices, with a wide variety of applications, including protection, healing, love, and prosperity. These aromatic and soothing mixtures typically consist of a blend of essential oils, herbs, and a base, such as beeswax or a plant-based oil like coconut or almond oil. Balms can be used for anointing candles, tools, and oneself, or incorporated into rituals, meditation, and spellwork. Creating your own balms allows you to customize the ingredients and intentions, providing a personal and powerful addition to your magical practice.

To begin creating a balm, start by selecting the base. Beeswax is a popular choice for its natural, solidifying properties, and its connection to the element of air, representing communication and transformation. Alternatively, you may choose a plant-based oil, such as almond, coconut, or jojoba oil, each with their own unique properties and correspondences. The base serves as a carrier for the essential oils and herbs, providing a stable medium for the mixture.

Next, choose the essential oils and herbs that align with your intentions and the purpose of the balm. Research the properties and correspondences of each ingredient and consider their synergistic effects when combined, I've outlined a few of these properties earlier in the book. For example, lavender is known for its calming and soothing properties, while rosemary is associated with protection and purification. It's important to ensure that the chosen oils and herbs are skin-safe and non-irritating.

Once you have selected your ingredients, begin by melting the beeswax or warming the plant-based oil in a double boiler over low heat. While the base is warming, combine the essential oils and herbs in a separate container, carefully measuring and blending to create a harmonious and balanced mixture. As you combine the ingredients, focus on your intentions and infuse the mixture with your desired energies.

When the base is fully melted or warmed, carefully add the essential oil and herb mixture, stirring gently to incorporate. Be cautious when handling the hot base, as it can cause burns. Continue to stir the mixture until it is well combined and uniform in consistency.

Pour the warm balm mixture into a heatproof container, such as a glass jar or tin, and allow it to cool and solidify. As the balm cools, take a moment to bless and consecrate it, infusing it with your intentions and purpose. You may choose to say a prayer, chant, or perform a simple ritual to empower the balm.

Once the balm has solidified, it is ready for use in your magical practice. Apply the balm to candles, tools, or yourself during rituals, meditation, or spellwork, focusing on the intentions and energies you infused into the mixture. Store the balm in a cool, dark place, and be mindful of its shelf life, as natural ingredients can degrade over time.

By creating your own balms for magical purposes, you are able to customize and imbue each blend with your personal energy and intentions, resulting in a powerful and meaningful addition to your practice. Experiment with different ingredients and combinations to discover the unique properties and effects of each blend and enjoy the process of crafting your own magical tools.

Wand Making

Discovering a fallen branch in the woods can be the beginning of a beautiful journey in crafting a personal and powerful magical wand. A wand is an extension of your will and energy, serving as a conduit for directing and focusing your intentions during spellwork, rituals, and meditation. The process of creating your own wand from a found branch allows you to form a deep and meaningful connection with the tool and the natural world from which it came.

When searching for a suitable branch, consider the type of tree from which it has fallen. Each tree species carries its own unique energy and symbolism, which will influence the properties of your wand. For example, oak is associated with strength, wisdom, and protection, while willow is known for its connection to intuition, dreams, and the moon. Allow your intuition to guide you in selecting a branch that resonates with your personal energy and magical practice.

Once you have found the perfect branch, take a moment to give thanks to the tree and the earth for providing this gift. You may choose to leave a small offering or simply express your gratitude with a silent prayer or intention. This act of gratitude strengthens your connection to the natural world and infuses your wand with positive energy.

Begin crafting your wand by carefully removing any leaves, twigs, or rough patches from the branch. You may use a knife or sandpaper to smooth and shape the wood, taking care to work with the natural curves and features of the branch. As you work, focus on your intentions for the wand and visualize the energy flowing through it.

Once the branch has been shaped and smoothed, you can choose to add personal touches and embellishments to enhance its beauty and power. Carving symbols, runes, or sigils into the wood can imbue the wand with specific energies and intentions. You may also choose to adorn your wand with crystals, feathers, or beads that hold personal significance or correspond to the wand's purpose. Attaching these items with natural materials such as twine, leather, or sinew further connects your wand to the earth and its energies.

After completing your wand, take the time to cleanse and consecrate it, preparing it for use in your magical practice. This can be done through smudging with sage, immersing it in moonlight, or placing it on an altar with intention. As you cleanse and consecrate your wand, focus on the energy and purpose you wish to imbue it with, and envision it as a powerful extension of your will.

Once your wand is ready, incorporate it into your magical practice, using it to direct and focus your energy during rituals, spellwork, and meditation. Your handcrafted wand will serve as a potent reminder of your connection to the natural world and the power of intention in shaping your magical practice.

Book of Shadows

Creating your own Book of Shadows is a deeply personal and empowering journey, allowing you to document your spiritual growth, magical knowledge, and experiences as you progress along your path. A Book of Shadows, sometimes referred to as a Grimoire, serves as a personal record of your beliefs, rituals, spells, and reflections, acting as both a guide and a source of inspiration. This sacred book can become a treasured heirloom, passed down through generations, preserving the wisdom and insights of your magical lineage.

When beginning your Book of Shadows, consider the type of book or journal you would like to use. Some practitioners prefer a bound book with blank pages, while others may opt for a binder or digital format that allows for easy organization and modification. Choose a medium that resonates with your personal style and preferences, and one that you will enjoy working with over time.

As you start to fill the pages of your Book of Shadows, think about the elements you wish to include. Many practitioners begin by recording their beliefs, spiritual or ethical codes, and personal insights on various aspects of magic and spirituality. This foundation provides a framework for your practice and a touchstone for future reflection.

One important aspect of your Book of Shadows is documenting your rituals and spells. This may include step-by-step instructions, ingredients or tools required, and any relevant correspondences, such as colors, herbs, crystals, or astrological influences. Over time, this section of your book will become a valuable resource, offering guidance and inspiration as you develop your magical practice.

In addition to rituals and spells, your Book of Shadows can also serve as a record of your personal experiences and reflections. This may include accounts of dreams, visions, or intuitive insights, as well as notes on your magical workings and their outcomes. By recording these experiences, you create a rich tapestry of your spiritual journey, allowing you to track your growth and progress over time.

Your Book of Shadows can also include sections on magical correspondences, such as herbs, crystals, colors, and symbols. These lists can serve as quick reference guides, helping you to select the appropriate tools and ingredients for your magical workings. Additionally, you may choose to include sections on divination, such as tarot, runes, or pendulum readings, providing a space to document your interpretations and insights.

Some practitioners also incorporate artwork, poetry, or other creative expressions into their Book of Shadows. These personal touches can help to make your book a true reflection of your unique spiritual path, imbuing it with your energy and intentions.

As your Book of Shadows grows, it may become a powerful tool in your rituals and magical workings. By regularly reviewing and reflecting on its contents, you can deepen your understanding of your practice and draw on the wisdom and insights you have gained over time. This sacred book can also serve as a source of inspiration, guidance, and support for future generations, providing a window into the magical traditions and experiences of their ancestors.

In crafting your own Book of Shadows, you create a living record of your spiritual journey, a testament to your growth and development as a practitioner of magic. By documenting your beliefs, rituals, spells, and reflections, you not only preserve your knowledge and insights for future generations but also develop a deeper understanding of your own practice, strengthening your connection to the magic within and around you.

Wildcrafted Vinegar

You can create one-of-a-kind homemade herbal infused vinegar by using almost any edible herb or plant to make herbal your own herbal tinctures. Herbal vinegars not only add concentrated flavor and acidity to your cooking but can also serve as a potential source of medicinal benefits. Since food is medicine, most common culinary herbs possess medicinal properties. For instance, rosemary can alleviate nausea, while thyme can relieve sinus congestion. Garlic boosts immunity, while ginger improves blood circulation. Cinnamon aids in sugar metabolism, and turmeric possesses natural anti-inflammatory properties. In addition to the medicinal properties of common culinary herbs, you can also explore the benefits of using medicinal plants, flowers, and wild edible weeds to create homemade infused vinegars. This opens up a vast array of options for crafting delicious and healing herbal vinegars that might not typically find their way into the kitchen.

While there are many recipes available for herbal vinegars in books and online, experimenting is often necessary when it comes to using wild herbs. It can be helpful to start with small batches and adjust the amount of herb used to find the right balance of flavor and medicinal benefit. Additionally, it's important to properly identify and research any wild herbs before using them in herbal vinegars to ensure safety and effectiveness.

Living in Alabama offers an array of opportunities to discover new and unique herbs to incorporate into my own culinary creations. I love exploring the diverse ecosystems and sourcing wild herbs, and growing my own herbs has been a satisfying way to ensure a steady supply of fresh and flavorful ingredients for my herbal vinegars.

If your initial attempts at using local wild ingredients in your herbal vinegars don't yield desired results, don't get discouraged. Learning from mistakes is part of the journey, and with practice and experimentation, you can create truly remarkable gourmet vinegars that showcase the unique flavors and medicinal benefits of wild herbs.

Vinegar options for making Herbal Vinegar

Unpasteurized apple cider vinegar (with "the mother")
Balsamic vinegar
Red wine vinegar
Sherry vinegar
Rice wine vinegar
Distilled white vinegar
White wine vinegar
Champagne vinegar
Ume plum vinegar

What to Extract with Vinegar

There are numerous ingredients that can be extracted with vinegar, and the possibilities are endless. However, I personally prefer to use herbs and fruits for my extracts. When deciding which ingredients to use for vinegar extracts,

147

seasonal availability can be a helpful guide. Popular options include sage, rosemary, elderberries, blueberries, and strawberries, among many others. When using fresh herbs for vinegar extracts, it's important to wash them thoroughly to remove any dirt or debris, and then pat them dry to remove excess moisture. This helps to prevent dilution of the vinegar and the growth of bacteria in the extract. When using fruits, you can choose to use them fresh or dried, but it's important to avoid using frozen fruits or previously frozen ones because they have a higher water content due to the formation of ice crystals. This can affect the quality and shelf life of the vinegar extract. Other botanicals like astragalus yarrow, chives, scallions, shallots, mustard, dill, horseradish, motherwort, lemon verbena, and dandelion leaves, flowers or roots can also be used to make vinegar extracts. It all depends on the desired flavor and medicinal properties.

Methods of Herbal Vinegar Infusion

When infusing herbs and stems in vinegar, the choice between using the hot or cold method depends solely on the flavors. For herbs like thyme and mugwort, the Hot Method Procedure tends to yield better flavor extraction, whereas herbs such as pineapple weed, basil, and mint fare better with the Cold Method Procedure. However, for pine, fir, spruce needles, and juniper berries, the Hot Method Procedure is not recommended as it can drastically alter their natural flavors.

The yield of your vinegar extract will vary depending on the size of the container used for infusion. You can adjust the quantity of ingredients according to your needs. If using fresh herbs, use a ratio of 2 parts organic vinegar to 1 part fresh organic fruit, herb, root, bark, or a combination of these. For
148

dried herbs, use a ratio of 1 part dried organic herb to 15 parts vinegar. For instance, if using a pint jar, add 2 tablespoons of dried herb and fill the rest of the jar with vinegar.

Extraction Tools

To ensure a seamless process while making vinegar extractions, it's important to have all the necessary equipment on hand. Due to the acidic nature of vinegar, it's recommended to use glass jars instead of plastic to avoid leaching. Before starting, sterilize your jars by boiling them in water for 10 minutes. Wide mouth jars are preferred for easy removal of the ingredients. Other essential items include cheesecloth, a fine mesh strainer, parchment paper, rubber bands, sharpie markers, and labels to ensure a safe and well-labeled end product.

Hot Method

The Hot Method Herbal Vinegar Procedure involves heating the vinegar and herbs together in a pot to extract the flavors. Here are the steps to follow:

Heat the vinegar in a non-reactive pot until it's hot but not boiling.

Remove the pot from heat and add the herbs.

Cover the pot and let it sit for several hours or overnight.

Strain the herbs from the vinegar using a fine-mesh strainer or cheesecloth.

Bottle the infused vinegar and store it in a cool, dark place.

149

Note: It's important to use non-reactive pots and utensils when making herbal vinegars to prevent any unwanted flavors or chemical reactions. Additionally, when heating the vinegar, be sure not to boil it as this can alter the flavors and acidity.

Cold Method

The Cold Method Herbal Vinegar Procedure involves steeping the herbs in vinegar at room temperature for several weeks. Here are the steps to follow:

Fill a glass jar with the herbs of your choice.

Cover the herbs completely with vinegar, making sure there's at least an inch of vinegar above the herbs.

Close the jar tightly and shake it to mix the ingredients.

Store the jar in a cool, dark place and let it steep for several weeks, shaking it occasionally.

Strain the herbs from the vinegar using a fine-mesh strainer or cheesecloth.

Bottle the infused vinegar and store it in a cool, dark place.

Note: The Cold Method Procedure requires more time and patience than the Hot Method, but it's gentler on the herbs and results in a more delicate flavor.

Healing Teas

Herbal teas have been used for centuries as a natural remedy to various ailments, from easing digestion issues to reducing anxiety and stress. Herbal teas are made from a combination of herbs, spices, and other natural ingredients, which work together to provide the desired benefits. Below is an essay on how to make healing herbal teas.

To begin with, it is important to choose high-quality herbs for your teas. The fresher the herbs, the better the tea will taste and the more potent the health benefits will be. It is best to grow your own or purchase organic herbs whenever possible to ensure they are free from pesticides and other harmful chemicals. I get all of my herbs that I can't grow myself from Mountain Rose Herbs.

Once you have chosen your herbs, you can begin to experiment with different combinations to find the perfect blend for your needs. For example, chamomile, lavender, and lemon balm are excellent herbs to use for a relaxing and calming tea, while ginger, peppermint, and fennel are great for aiding digestion.

To make a healing herbal tea, start by boiling water in a kettle or on the stove. While the water is heating up, prepare your herbs by washing them thoroughly and chopping them into small pieces. You can use a tea infuser or a mesh strainer to hold the herbs while steeping.

Once the water has come to a boil, remove it from the heat and let it cool for a minute or two before pouring it over the herbs. Let the tea steep for 5-10 minutes, or until it reaches your desired strength. The longer the tea steeps, the stronger it will be.

When the tea is ready, strain out the herbs and discard them. You can sweeten the tea with honey or another natural sweetener, if desired. Sip the tea slowly, enjoying the aroma and flavor while allowing the healing properties to work their magic.

Herbal teas are a simple and effective way to incorporate natural healing into your daily routine. Experiment with different herbs and combinations to find the perfect blend for your needs. By making healing herbal teas a part of your daily routine, you can experience the many benefits of natural medicine and support your overall health and well-being.

Warning: These recipes are not for use in pregnancy except under the supervision of a qualified healthcare practitioner. Consult with a qualified healthcare practitioner before consuming herbal products, particularly if you are pregnant, nursing, or on any medications.

This information has not been evaluated by the Food and Drug Administration. This information is not intended to diagnose, treat, cure, or prevent any disease and is for spiritual and educational purposes only.

These herbal ingredients was hand selected by me and can be a great addition to a kitchen witch's repertoire when it comes to creating love and enchantment.

Red Rooibos: Red Rooibos is a South African herbal tea that is known for its calming and soothing properties. It's often used to help reduce stress and anxiety, which can be beneficial when it comes to creating a peaceful and loving atmosphere.

Honeybush: Honeybush is another South African herbal tea that has a sweet, honey-like flavor. It's believed to promote harmony and balance in relationships, making it a great choice for a love potion.

Raspberry Leaf: Raspberry Leaf has been used for centuries in traditional medicine to promote fertility and enhance the chances of conception. It's also known for its ability to strengthen the uterus and balance hormones, which can be helpful for those looking to conceive or for those who want to enhance their romantic relationships.

Hibiscus: Hibiscus has a tart and tangy flavor and is known for its ability to promote love, passion, and sensuality. It's often used in love spells and potions to help increase desire and attraction.

Roses: Roses have been associated with love and romance for centuries. They're often used in love potions and spells to enhance feelings of love, passion, and romance.

Cacao Nibs: Cacao nibs are small pieces of crushed cocoa beans and are known for their ability to promote feelings of happiness and euphoria. They're often used in love potions and spells to create a sense of pleasure and joy.

Carob: Carob is a sweet and nutty tasting powder that is often used as a chocolate substitute. It's believed to have a calming effect on the mind and body, making it a great choice for promoting love and relaxation.

Cinnamon Chips: Cinnamon chips are a warm and aromatic spice that is often used in love potions and spells to enhance feelings of love, attraction, and passion. It's believed to have a fiery and passionate energy that can help to stimulate the senses and promote desire.

Here's my recipe for this enchanting tea blend.

Ingredients:

2 parts red rooibos

1 part honeybush

1 part raspberry Leaf

1/2 part hibiscus

1/4 part rose nibs

1/4 part cacao nibs

1/4 part carob

1/4 part cinnamon chips

Instructions:

Combine all the ingredients in a mixing bowl, and stir gently to blend them together.

Store the mixture in an airtight container, and keep it in a cool, dry place.

To make a cup of tea, boil water in a kettle, and pour it over 1-2 teaspoons of the tea blend.

Steep the tea for 5-7 minutes, then strain the tea leaves and enjoy. Add honey or your favorite sweetener.

This tea blend is a perfect balance of flavors, with the earthy and nutty notes of Red Rooibos and Honeybush, the tartness of Hibiscus and Raspberry Leaf, and the sweetness of Roses, Cacao Nibs, Carob, and Cinnamon Chips.

Through the Looking Glass Divination Tea

Perfect for sipping during Tarot readings or other divination work, this Divination Tea is a handcrafted blend of herbs that have historically been used to enhance clairvoyance and psychic ability.

Ingredients:

1 part damiana
1 part dandelion root

1 part mugwort

1 part lemon balm

1/2 part hibiscus

1/2 part peppermint

A sprinkle of roses

Instructions:

Combine all the ingredients in a mixing bowl, and stir gently to blend them together.

Store the mixture in an airtight container, and keep it in a cool, dry place.

To make a cup of tea, boil water in a kettle, and pour it over 1-2 teaspoons of the tea blend.

Steep the tea for 5-7 minutes, then strain the tea leaves and enjoy.

Honey & lemon or cinnamon may be added for flavor.

Here's the properties of each ingredient and how they can aid in divination:

Damiana: Damiana is a herb known for its aphrodisiac properties, but it can also be helpful in divination. It's believed to help connect with one's intuition and enhance psychic abilities.

Dandelion Root: Dandelion Root is a cleansing herb that can help to purify the body and mind, making it easier to receive messages from the spiritual realm.

Mugwort: Mugwort is a powerful herb for divination, known for its ability to enhance psychic powers, increase clarity, and stimulate prophetic dreams.

Lemon Balm: Lemon Balm is a calming herb that can help to reduce stress and anxiety, making it easier to focus and tune in to one's intuition.

Hibiscus: Hibiscus is known for its ability to promote intuition and spiritual awareness. It's believed to help open the third eye chakra, which can facilitate access to higher realms of consciousness.

Peppermint: Peppermint is a refreshing herb that can help to clear the mind and stimulate mental clarity, making it easier to receive and interpret messages from the spiritual realm.

Roses: Roses are often associated with love and romance, but they can also be helpful in divination. They're believed to enhance psychic abilities and promote spiritual insight, making them a great addition to a divination tea blend.

By combining these herbs in a tea blend, you can create a powerful brew that can aid in divination and help you to connect with your intuition and the spiritual realm.

Daydreamer's Calming Tea

The Daydreamer Calming Tea Blend was handcrafted to create a perfect cloud-top calm moment. Designed with ingredients historically used for relaxing and calming for your moments of wellness.

Ingredients:

1 part Chamomile
1 part Lemon Balm
1/2 part Holy Basil
1/2 part Passionflower
1/2 part Rose Petals
1/2 part Lavender

Instructions:

Combine all the ingredients in a mixing bowl, and stir gently to blend them together.

Store the mixture in an airtight container, and keep it in a cool, dry place.

To make a cup of tea, boil water in a kettle, and pour it over 1-2 teaspoons of the tea blend.

Steep the tea for 5-7 minutes, then strain the tea leaves and add honey or lemon to taste.

Now, let's explore the properties of each ingredient and how they can aid in promoting calmness and relaxation:

Chamomile: Chamomile is a gentle herb that is often used to promote relaxation and sleep. It's believed to have a calming effect on the mind and body, making it a great choice for a calming tea.

Lemon Balm: Lemon Balm is a calming herb that can help to reduce stress and anxiety. It's believed to have a soothing effect on the nervous system, which can help to promote relaxation.

Holy Basil: Holy Basil, also known as Tulsi, is a herb that is often used in Ayurvedic medicine to promote relaxation and reduce stress. It's believed to have a calming effect on the mind and body, and can help to reduce anxiety and promote mental clarity.

Passionflower: Passionflower is a herb known for its ability to promote relaxation and sleep. It's believed to have a sedative effect on the nervous system, which can help to reduce anxiety and promote restful sleep.

Rose Petals: Rose petals are often associated with love and romance, but they can also be helpful in promoting relaxation. They're believed to have a calming effect on the mind and body, and can help to reduce stress and anxiety.

Lavender: Lavender is a calming herb that is often used to promote relaxation and reduce stress. It's believed to have a soothing effect on the nervous system, and can help to promote restful sleep.

By combining these herbs in a tea blend, you can create a soothing and calming brew that can help to promote relaxation and reduce stress and anxiety. Adding honey or lemon can provide added flavor and sweetness, making it a delicious and comforting drink. Enjoy your calming tea and take some time to relax and unwind.

Note: Peppermint might be an option for you to add to this blend, however it's not for me. I find it to be too stimulating for a calming blend. It is a popular herb that is often added to tea blends for its refreshing and invigorating flavor. While it is known for its energizing properties, it can also have a calming effect on the body and mind. Peppermint contains a compound called menthol, which has a relaxing effect on the muscles and can help to reduce tension and promote relaxation. It also has a cooling and soothing effect on the digestive system, which can help to ease feelings of nausea or discomfort that can be associated with stress and anxiety. However, as I mentioned, some people may find peppermint to be too strong or stimulating, especially if you are particularly sensitive to its effects. In this case, it may be best to leave it out of a calming tea blend and instead focus on other herbs that are better suited to your individual needs and preferences.

Aurora's Sleep Tea

The Aurora Sleep Tea Deep Sleep Blend is a handcrafted blend of herbs that have historically been used to aid in insomnia and for a deep sleep.

Ingredients:

1 part valerian root
1 part lemon balm
1 part passionflower
1 part skullcap
1/2 part lavender
1/2 part roses

Instructions:

Combine all the ingredients in a mixing bowl and stir gently to blend them together.

Store the mixture in an airtight container, and keep it in a cool, dry place.

To make a cup of tea, boil water in a kettle, and pour it over 1-2 teaspoons of the tea blend.

Steep the tea for 5-7 minutes, then strain the tea leaves. Honey & lemon or cinnamon may be added for flavor. Drink 30 minutes before bedtime.

Properties of each ingredient and how they can aid in promoting restful sleep:

Valerian Root: Valerian is an herb that is often used to promote relaxation and sleep. It's believed to have a sedative effect on the nervous system, which can help to promote restful sleep.

Lemon Balm: Lemon Balm is a calming herb that can help to reduce stress and anxiety. It's believed to have a soothing effect on the nervous system, which can help to promote relaxation and restful sleep.

Passionflower: Passionflower is an herb known for its ability to promote relaxation and sleep. It's believed to have a sedative effect on the nervous system, which can help to reduce anxiety and promote restful sleep.

Skullcap: Skullcap is a calming herb that can help to promote relaxation and reduce feelings of anxiety. It's believed to have a calming effect on the nervous system, which can help to promote restful sleep.

Lavender: Lavender is a calming herb that is often used to promote relaxation and reduce stress. It's believed to have a soothing effect on the nervous system and can help to promote restful sleep.

Roses: Roses are often associated with love and romance, but they can also be helpful in promoting relaxation. They're believed to have a calming effect on the mind and body and can help to reduce stress and anxiety.

By combining these herbs in a tea blend, you can create a calming and relaxing brew that can help to promote restful sleep. Drinking this tea 30 minutes before bedtime can help to calm the mind and body, making it easier to fall asleep and stay asleep throughout the night. Enjoy your sleep tea and wake up feeling refreshed and rejuvenated.

Golden Goddess Awakening Tea

Awaken the Golden Goddess within with this fragrant Freya Inspired tea blend. Freya is a Norse goddess associated with beauty, love, and fertility, and is often depicted with a radiant, golden aura. This awakening tea blend was inspired by her qualities of radiance, vitality, and beauty. The bright colors of hibiscus and calendula flowers in the blend evoke the golden aura of Freya, while the energizing and also calming properties of the other ingredients can help to radiate beauty, love, and success. Enjoy a cup of this tea and let the golden energy of Freya inspire and uplift you.

Ingredients:

2 parts Hibiscus
1 part Lemongrass
1 part Lemon Balm
1/2 part Calendula Flowers
1/2 part Orange Peel
Instructions:

163

Combine all the ingredients in a mixing bowl and stir gently to blend them together.

Store the mixture in an airtight container, and keep it in a cool, dry place.

To make a cup of tea, boil water in a kettle, and pour it over 1-2 teaspoons of the tea blend.

Steep the tea for 5-7 minutes, then strain the tea leaves and enjoy. Honey & lemon may be added for flavor.

Properties of each ingredient and how they are good for awakening:

Hibiscus: Hibiscus is known for its tart, fruity flavor and is a great source of antioxidants. It's believed to help promote overall health and vitality, making it a great addition to an awakening blend.

Lemongrass: Lemongrass has a fresh, citrusy flavor and is known for its energizing properties. It can help to stimulate the mind and body, making it a great addition to a blend aimed at promoting success and radiating beauty.

Lemon Balm: Lemon balm is a calming herb that can help to reduce stress and anxiety. It's believed to have a soothing effect on the nervous system, making it a great addition to a blend aimed at promoting beauty and love.

Calendula Flowers: Calendula flowers are known for their bright, sunny appearance and have been used for centuries in traditional medicine for their healing properties. They're believed to help promote skin health and radiance, making them a great addition to a blend aimed at promoting beauty.

Orange Peel: Orange peel has a sweet, citrusy flavor and is a great source of vitamin C. It's believed to help promote overall health and wellness, making it a great addition to a blend aimed at promoting awakening and success.

By combining these ingredients in a tea blend, you can create a delicious and invigorating brew that can help to promote awakening, beauty, love, and success. Enjoy your tea and let its positive energy radiate throughout your day!

The Lovers Decadent Herbal Hot Chocolate

An elegant chocolate treat that tastes creamy and oh so chocolatey! "The Lovers" is an herbalist's take on your favorite winter warm up beverage while snuggling up after a day in the cold. This blend is as satisfying as hot chocolate - it is delicious and guilt-free! Packed full of nutritious herbs that will aid in boosting your immune system. My blend uses no dried milk for those who want to substitute soy milk, coconut milk or any non-dairy product.

Ingredients:

2 tablespoons cocoa powder

1 teaspoon chaga powder

1 teaspoon maca powder

1 teaspoon ashwagandha powder

1 tablespoon coconut sugar

2 cups non-dairy milk (such as almond, coconut, or soy milk)

Instructions:

In a small mixing bowl, combine the cocoa powder, chaga powder, maca powder, ashwagandha powder, and coconut sugar, and stir until well blended.

In a small saucepan, heat the non-dairy milk over medium heat until it begins to steam.

Add the cocoa powder mixture to the saucepan and whisk until the ingredients are well combined.

Continue to whisk the mixture until it begins to thicken and become frothy.

Remove the saucepan from the heat and pour the hot cocoa into two mugs.

Serve immediately, and enjoy your delicious, herbal hot cocoa with someone you love.

Properties of each ingredient and how they can contribute to the taste and health benefits of the hot cocoa:

Cocoa Powder: Cocoa powder is the base of this hot cocoa recipe, providing a rich, chocolatey flavor that we all know and love. Cocoa powder also contains flavonoids, which are antioxidants that can help to protect the body against oxidative stress.

Chaga Powder: Chaga is a type of mushroom that's rich in antioxidants and can help to support the immune system. It has a slightly earthy flavor that pairs well with the cocoa powder.

Maca Powder: Maca is a root vegetable that's often ground into a powder and used as a natural remedy for hormonal balance and energy. It has a slightly nutty flavor that can add depth to the cocoa powder.

Ashwagandha Powder: Ashwagandha is an adaptogenic herb that can help to reduce stress and anxiety. It has a slightly bitter taste that can be balanced out by the sweetness of the coconut sugar.

Coconut Sugar: Coconut sugar is a natural sweetener that's lower in glycemic index than regular sugar. It has a caramel-like flavor that pairs well with the cocoa powder and other ingredients.

By combining these ingredients in a hot cocoa recipe, you can create a delicious and nourishing treat that can provide a natural energy boost and support your overall health and well-being. Enjoy your herbal hot cocoa, and feel free to experiment with different proportions of the ingredients to find your perfect blend.

Waking the Dead Herbal Coffee Substitute

This Herbal Coffee was created for coffee lovers and is packed full of immune boosters and detoxifying herbs and will provide a consistent level of energy without the caffeine crash.

Ingredients:

1/4 cup Roasted Chicory Root
1/4 cup Roasted Dandelion Root
1 tbsp Ashwagandha Powder
1 tbsp Burdock Root
1 tsp Cinnamon Powder
1 tbsp Carob Powder
1 tsp Chaga Powder
1 tsp Maca Powder

Instructions:

In a large bowl, mix together the roasted chicory root, roasted dandelion root, ashwagandha powder, burdock root, cinnamon powder, carob powder, chaga powder, and maca powder until well combined.

Store the mixture in an airtight container until ready to use.

To make Herbal Coffee, add 1-2 tablespoons of the Herbal Coffee mixture to a French press or coffee maker.

Pour hot water over the mixture, and steep for 15-20 minutes for medium roast and 25-30 minutes for dark roast

Strain the Herbal Coffee into a mug, and enjoy!

Properties of each ingredient and how they contribute to the flavor and health benefits of this Herbal Coffee:

Roasted Chicory Root: Chicory root is a popular coffee substitute that has a nutty, slightly bitter flavor. It's rich in inulin, a type of soluble fiber that can help to support digestive health.

Roasted Dandelion Root: Dandelion root is another coffee substitute that has a similar flavor profile to chicory root. It's a natural diuretic and can help to support liver health.

Ashwagandha Powder: Ashwagandha is an adaptogenic herb that can help to reduce stress and anxiety. It has a slightly bitter taste that can be balanced out by the sweetness of the carob powder.

Burdock Root: Burdock root is a natural detoxifier that can help to support liver health. It has a slightly earthy taste that pairs well with the other ingredients.

Cinnamon Powder: Cinnamon is a warming spice that can help to improve blood sugar control and reduce inflammation.

Carob Powder: Carob is a natural sweetener that's low in caffeine and rich in antioxidants. It has a sweet, chocolatey flavor that can mimic the taste of coffee.

Chaga Powder: Chaga is a type of mushroom that's rich in antioxidants and can help to support the immune system. It has a slightly earthy flavor that pairs well with the other ingredients.

Maca Powder: Maca is a root vegetable that's often ground into a powder and used as a natural remedy for hormonal balance and energy. It has a slightly nutty flavor that can add depth to the Herbal Coffee.

By combining these ingredients in an Herbal Coffee recipe, you can create a delicious and nourishing alternative to traditional coffee that can support your overall health and well-being. Experiment with different proportions of the ingredients to find your perfect blend and enjoy!

My Signature Tea Blends

Maiden, Mother, and Crone

It's important that we celebrate and support women in all cycles of life. My Goddess inspired Triple Goddess Collection supports women in all stages in their journey through the phases of Maiden, Mother, and Crone. These blends are handcrafted with historically used ingredients to offer support for mensuration, motherhood, and menopause.

Persephone's (Maiden) Blend

The Persephone blend is a supportive tea blend for women during their monthly moon cycle. This blend is inspired by The Maiden and the New Moon and is handcrafted to offer support and alleviate symptoms during mensuration. Each ingredient has been carefully chosen for its unique properties that work together to alleviate symptoms such as cramping and stress and promote physical and emotional ease. Red clover and cramp bark are known for their ability to ease menstrual cramps, while dandelion leaf helps to support the liver and promote detoxification. Holy basil and St. John's Wort help to reduce stress and anxiety, and nettle is a great source of iron and other essential nutrients. Chamomile, roses, and lavender provide a calming and soothing effect on the mind and body, making this blend the perfect companion for young maidens during their time of the month.

Ingredients:

2 parts red clover

2 parts cramp bark

2 parts dandelion leaf

1 part holy basil

1 part St. John's Wort

1 part nettle

1 part chamomile

1 part roses

1 part lavender

Instructions:

Combine all the herbs in a large mixing bowl.

Mix thoroughly to ensure that all the herbs are evenly distributed. Store the blend in an airtight container in a cool, dark place.

Add 1 teaspoon to 6 oz boiling water and steep for 5-10 minutes. Begin drinking 7-10 days before your cycle begins and continue throughout the week. Shake well before use and add black strap molasses

Demeter's (Mother) Blend

The Demeter Blend is crafted to support women transitioning into motherhood . Whether she is welcoming her first baby or fourth every mom deserves love and self care. Each ingredient has been chosen for its unique properties that work together to provide nourishment, hydration, and relaxation. Raspberry leaf is a well-known herb for its ability to support the uterus and promote a healthy pregnancy. Lemon balm and lady's mantle are gentle herbal allies that help to calm the nervous system and reduce anxiety. Nettle leaf is a great source of essential nutrients, while chamomile and peppermint provide a soothing and relaxing effect. Rose petals and lavender add a touch of sweetness and a pleasant aroma to the blend. Enjoy a cup of the Demeter blend to show love and care for yourself as you navigate this special time in your life.

Ingredients:

2 parts raspberry leaf
2 parts lemon balm
2 parts lady's mantle
1 part nettle leaf
1 part chamomile
1 part peppermint
1 part rose petals
1 part lavender

Instructions:

Combine all the herbs in a large mixing bowl.

Mix thoroughly to ensure that all the herbs are evenly distributed. Store the blend in an airtight container in a cool, dark place.

Add 1 teaspoon to 6 oz boiling water and steep for 5-10 minutes. Add honey for taste

Hecate's (Crone) Blend

The Hecate blend is a supportive tea blend inspired by The Crone, the Dark Mother Hecate, and the Dark Moon. This blend is crafted for women going through menopause. This blend is formulated to offer support throughout your journey and all of the changes this transition brings. I hand selected historically used ingredients to empower with love, marriage, creativity, divination, protection, strength, courage, transmutation, wisdom, healing, preserving, vitality, purpose, joy, success. This blend will offer spiritual nourishment and balance. The raspberry leaf in this blend has historically been used to support the female reproductive system and alleviate cramping. Lady's mantle is believed to offer protection and healing, while milk thistle helps to cleanse and protect the liver. Nettles are a nourishing herb that can support the body during times of change, and black cohosh root is known for its ability to relieve hot flashes and other menopausal symptoms. Licorice root can help to balance hormones and support adrenal health, while motherwort is believed to offer emotional support during this time of transition. Peppermint is included for its soothing and calming properties, and Hawthorne berries are added for their ability to strengthen the heart and circulatory system. All of these herbs work together to create a supportive and nourishing blend for women going through menopause.

Ingredients:

174

1 tbsp raspberry leaf

1 tbsp lady's mantle

1 tbsp milk thistle

1 tbsp nettles

1 tsp black cohosh root

1 tsp licorice root

1 tsp motherwort

1 tsp peppermint

a few hawthorne berries

Instructions:

Mix all of the herbs together in a bowl.

Place 1 tablespoon of the mixture in a tea infuser or strainer.

Boil water and pour it over the herbs.

Let the tea steep for 5-10 minutes.

Add honey for taste.

Remove the tea infuser or strainer and enjoy!

Bath Scrubs

Bath scrubs have been used for centuries to promote relaxation, rejuvenation, and physical and emotional well-being. Regenerating bath salts can help revitalize the body, improve circulation, and promote healthy skin. These salts can be made with a combination of various minerals, herbs, and essential oils, and can be customized to suit individual needs and preferences.

To make regenerating bath salts, you will need an exfoliant like Epsom salt, Himalayan salt, sugar, coffee, or oatmeal. You will also need dried herbs and essential oils. Epsom salt is rich in magnesium, which helps relax muscles and reduce inflammation. Himalayan salt is packed with minerals and can help detoxify the body.

Sugar scrubs are made by mixing granulated sugar with a carrier oil, such as coconut oil or almond oil, and any desired essential oils or other natural ingredients. The sugar granules help to remove dead skin cells, while the carrier oil moisturizes the skin. Sugar scrubs are great for all skin types, but are especially beneficial for dry, flaky skin. They can also help to improve circulation and reduce the appearance of cellulite.

Coffee scrubs are another popular option for bath scrubs and are made using used coffee grounds mixed with a carrier oil and any desired essential oils. Coffee grounds are a great exfoliant, as they contain caffeine, which can help to improve circulation and reduce inflammation. They also contain antioxidants, which can help to protect the skin from damage caused by free radicals. Coffee scrubs are especially beneficial for oily or acne-prone skin, as they can help to unclog pores and reduce the appearance of blemishes.

In addition to sugar and coffee, there are many other natural ingredients that can be used to create bath scrubs. For example, salt scrubs are made using sea salt or epsom salt, which provide a more intense exfoliation than sugar or coffee. Other popular ingredients for bath scrubs include oatmeal, which can help to soothe and nourish the skin, and honey, which is a natural humectant that helps to lock in moisture.

Dried herbs can provide additional benefits such as relaxation, skin nourishment, and aromatherapy. Essential oils can enhance the effects of the bath salts, promote relaxation, and provide a pleasant scent.

Start by combining equal parts Epsom salt and Himalayan salt in a mixing bowl. Mix well to ensure the salts are evenly distributed. Add a handful of dried herbs of your choice such as lavender, chamomile, rose petals, or calendula. Mix well to ensure the herbs are evenly distributed throughout the mixture.

Next, add 5-10 drops of your preferred essential oil. Some popular options include lavender, eucalyptus, peppermint, or citrus oils. Mix well to ensure the oil is evenly distributed. You can also add a few drops of food coloring if desired to give your bath salts a pop of color.

Once your bath salts are mixed, transfer them to an airtight container to prevent moisture from getting in. A mason jar or glass jar with a tight-fitting lid works well for storing bath salts.

To use your regenerating bath salts, simply add a handful or two to warm bathwater and soak for at least 20 minutes. The warm water will help dissolve the salts and release the essential oils and herbs into the water, creating a relaxing and rejuvenating experience.

When making your own bath scrubs, it's important to choose high-quality, natural ingredients, as well as to avoid any ingredients that may be irritating to your skin. It's also important to store your scrubs in a cool, dry place, and to use them within a few weeks of making them to ensure that they are fresh and effective.

Herbal bath scrubs are another great option for those looking to incorporate natural ingredients into their self-care routine. Herbs such as lavender, chamomile, and calendula are known for their soothing and calming properties. They can help to reduce inflammation, improve skin hydration, and promote relaxation. Herbal bath scrubs can also be made with dried herbs and salts, providing an added boost of minerals and nutrients for the skin. Essential oils can also enhance the benefits of your bath scrubs. Lavender oil, for example, is known for its calming and relaxing properties, while peppermint oil can help to invigorate the senses and improve circulation. Tea tree oil is a great choice for those with acne-prone skin, as it has natural antibacterial properties.

Whether you prefer bath salts, sugar scrubs, coffee scrubs, herbal scrubs, or a combination of these into your self-care routine, this can be a great way to incorporate natural ingredients into your self-care into your routine. You can nourish and rejuvenate your skin while also promoting relaxation and well-being.

Energizing Citrus Scrub

Ingredients:

1 cup of white sugar
1/2 cup of coconut oil
1/4 cup of dried orange peel
1/4 cup of dried lemon zest
10 drops of grapefruit essential oil
1 tbsp of dried rosemary

Directions:

In a mixing bowl, combine the white sugar and coconut oil until it forms a paste.

Add the dried orange peel and lemon zest to the mixture and stir until it is evenly distributed.

Add 10 drops of grapefruit essential oil and stir again.

Finally, mix in a tablespoon of dried rosemary.

To use the scrub, apply a small amount to your skin in a circular motion, paying extra attention to dry or rough areas. Rinse off with warm water.

Properties of each ingredient:

Orange Peel: Rich in vitamin C and antioxidants, orange peel helps to rejuvenate and brighten the skin. It also has a refreshing citrus scent that can help to invigorate the senses.

Lemon Zest: Also rich in vitamin C and antioxidants, lemon zest helps to exfoliate and cleanse the skin, while its uplifting scent can help to boost energy levels.

Grapefruit Essential Oil: Known for its energizing and mood-lifting properties, grapefruit essential oil can help to promote feelings of happiness and vitality. It also has antiseptic and antibacterial properties, making it a great addition to a bath scrub.

Coconut Oil: A natural moisturizer, coconut oil helps to nourish and hydrate the skin, leaving it soft and supple.

Rosemary: This fragrant herb is known for its stimulating and revitalizing properties. It can help to improve circulation and ease muscle tension, while its fresh scent can help to clear the mind and increase focus.

Soothing Lavender Scrub

Ingredients:

1/2 cup dried lavender buds
1/2 cup oatmeal

1/4 cup almond oil

1/2 cup Epsom salt

Instructions:

In a bowl, mix together the dried lavender buds and oatmeal.

Add in the almond oil and mix until everything is well combined.

Stir in the Epsom salt until fully incorporated.

Transfer the mixture to a jar or container for storage.

Properties of each ingredient:

Lavender buds: Lavender is a well-known herb for its soothing and calming properties, making it perfect for a relaxing bath scrub. Its aroma helps to reduce stress and anxiety, promote better sleep, and alleviate headaches.

Oatmeal: Oatmeal is a gentle exfoliant that helps to remove dead skin cells and soothe dry, irritated skin. It also contains anti-inflammatory properties that can help to reduce redness and itching.

Almond oil: Almond oil is rich in vitamin E and fatty acids, making it an excellent moisturizer for the skin. It helps to hydrate and nourish the skin while also protecting it from damage caused by free radicals.

Epsom salt: Epsom salt is known for its ability to soothe sore muscles and promote relaxation. It also helps to exfoliate the skin and improve its texture.

Exfoliating Coffee Scrub

Ingredients:

1 cup coffee grounds

1/2 cup brown sugar

1/2 cup coconut oil

1 tsp vanilla extract

Properties of ingredients:

Coffee grounds: The caffeine in coffee is known to have antioxidant properties, and it can help reduce inflammation and promote circulation in the skin. The texture of coffee grounds also helps exfoliate dead skin cells.

Brown sugar: Brown sugar is a natural exfoliant that can help remove dead skin cells and unclog pores. It also contains glycolic acid, which can help improve the overall texture of the skin.

Coconut oil: Coconut oil is moisturizing and can help nourish the skin. It also has antimicrobial properties that can help prevent infections.

Vanilla extract: Vanilla extract has a pleasant scent and can help relax the mind and body.

Instructions:

In a bowl, mix together the coffee grounds and brown sugar.

In a separate bowl, melt the coconut oil and mix in the vanilla extract.

Pour the coconut oil mixture into the bowl with the coffee and sugar mixture, and stir until well combined.

Transfer the scrub to a jar with a lid.

To use, wet your skin and apply the scrub in a circular motion, focusing on areas with rough skin or cellulite. Rinse off thoroughly with water.

Calming Chamomile Scrub

1/2 cup dried chamomile flowers
1/2 cup sea salt
1/4 cup honey
1/4 cup sweet almond oil

Instructions:

Grind the dried chamomile flowers in a food processor until they are a fine powder.

In a bowl, mix together the chamomile powder, sea salt, honey, and sweet almond oil.

Stir until the ingredients are well combined and form a paste-like consistency.

Store the scrub in an airtight container until ready to use.

Properties of each ingredient:

Chamomile is a calming herb that has been used for centuries to help soothe the mind and body. When used in a scrub, chamomile can help calm and relax the skin, making it perfect for a calming bath.

Sea salt in the scrub helps exfoliate the skin, removing dead skin cells and leaving it feeling soft and smooth.

Honey is a natural humectant, which means it helps retain moisture in the skin.

Sweet almond oil is rich in vitamin E, which helps nourish and protect the skin.

Together, these ingredients create a gentle and soothing scrub that is perfect for unwinding after a long day.

Matcha Scrub

This lavender matcha herbal sugar scrub is inspired by the delicious and popular lavender matcha latte. The sweet and earthy combination of matcha and lavender is not only pleasing to the taste buds but also nourishing to the skin. Matcha, a type of green tea, is known for its high levels of antioxidants that help protect the skin from damage and aging. Lavender, on the other hand, is a calming and soothing herb that can help reduce stress and promote relaxation. Together with the exfoliating properties of sugar and the cleansing effects of bentonite clay, this scrub is perfect for a luxurious and rejuvenating self-care experience.

Ingredients:

1/2 cup lavender herbal sugar

1/4 cup coconut oil

2 tablespoons matcha powder

2 tablespoons bentonite clay

a handful of dried lavender buds

Directions:

In a mixing bowl, combine the herbal sugar, matcha powder, and bentonite clay. Stir until well combined.

Add the dried lavender buds and mix again.

Gradually add in the coconut oil, stirring until the mixture becomes a smooth paste.

Transfer the scrub to a jar with a tight-fitting lid.

Description of Ingredients:

Matcha powder: Matcha is a type of green tea that is packed with antioxidants and caffeine, making it a great ingredient for energizing and brightening the skin.

Bentonite clay: This clay has detoxifying properties and helps draw out impurities from the skin.

Coconut oil: A natural moisturizer that helps hydrate and nourish the skin.

Lavender buds: Lavender has calming and soothing properties, which make it great for a relaxing and stress-relieving scrub.

Lavender herbal sugar: This infused sugar is a versatile and magical ingredient that can be used in various ways. Lavender, in general, is known for its calming and soothing properties, and is often used for protection, purification, love, and healing. When infused in sugar, it takes on the sweet and delicate scent of lavender, making it an ideal addition to various recipes like this one. This sugar can enhance your intentions for love, peace, and relaxation. It can also be used to sweeten spells or offerings to the gods and goddesses that resonate with your intention. The sugar component of the infusion adds a layer of sweetness and can also represent the element of earth, grounding and anchoring. I hope this scrub can help you connect with the calming and soothing energy while also adding a touch of sweetness to your magical bath.

Warming Cinnamon Scrub

Ingredients:

1 cup brown sugar
1 tablespoon cinnamon powder
1/2 cup olive oil
a few drops of ginger essential oil

Directions:

In a mixing bowl, combine brown sugar and cinnamon powder. Slowly pour in the olive oil and mix until it forms a thick paste. Transfer the mixture to an airtight container and store in a cool, dry place until ready to use.

To use, apply the scrub to damp skin and gently massage in a circular motion. Rinse off with warm water and pat dry. The cinnamon and brown sugar work together to exfoliate and remove dead skin cells, while the olive oil moisturizes and nourishes the skin.

This a a simple and invigorating scrub that's perfect for cold weather.

Cinnamon is known for its warming and energizing properties. It can help to increase circulation and stimulate the senses, making it a great addition to a body scrub.

Brown sugar is a natural humectant, meaning it helps to draw moisture to the skin, while

Olive oil is rich in antioxidants and essential fatty acids that can help to protect and repair the skin.

Together, these ingredients create a scrub that is both invigorating and nourishing for the skin.

Balancing Rose Scrub

Ingredients:

1/2 cup dried rose petals
1 cup Epsom salt
1/4 cup jojoba oil
10-15 drops of rose essential oil

Directions:

In a food processor, pulse the dried rose petals until they are broken down into small pieces.

In a mixing bowl, combine the rose petals with the Epsom salt and mix well.

Add the jojoba oil and rose essential oil to the mixture and stir until the ingredients are well combined.

Mix in a few rose petals.

Transfer the mixture to an airtight container for storage.

Magical Properties:

Roses have been used in herbalism for centuries for their skin-nourishing properties

Epsom salt is known for its detoxifying and exfoliating benefits

Jojoba oil is a natural moisturizer that won't clog pores

Rose essential oil adds a soothing, calming aroma to the scrub

Use this scrub in the bath or shower to pamper yourself, exfoliate and soften your skin, and to relax your mind and body with the scent of roses.

My Signature Scrubs

Siren's Dead Sea Salt Scrub

This Salt Scrub is a simple, all-natural body scrub that will leave your skin feeling soft, smooth, and rejuvenated. This scrub is designed to exfoliate and cleanse your skin, while the natural minerals in the Dead Sea salt help to nourish and rejuvenate your skin. The scrub is perfect for use before or during a bath, and its magical properties may help to enhance your connection to the element of water, making it an excellent addition to your self-care and spiritual rituals.

Ingredients:

1 cup Dead Sea salt

1/2 cup coconut oil, melted

1/4 cup almond oil

5 drops lavender essential oil

5 drops chamomile essential oil

Instructions:

In a medium-sized mixing bowl, combine the Dead Sea salt, melted coconut oil, and almond oil. Stir the ingredients together until they are well mixed and the salt is evenly coated in the oils.

Add the lavender and chamomile essential oils to the salt and oil mixture. Stir the ingredients together to ensure the essential oils are evenly distributed throughout the scrub.

Transfer the salt scrub to a clean, airtight container, such as a glass jar with a tight-fitting lid. Store the scrub in a cool, dry place, away from direct sunlight.

To use the scrub, scoop a small amount of the mixture into your hands and gently massage it onto your wet skin in circular motions. Focus on areas with dry or rough skin, such as elbows, knees, and feet. Rinse the scrub off with warm water and pat your skin dry with a clean towel.

Incorporate this scrub into your self-care routine or use it as part of a ritual bath to enhance your connection to the element of water and the energies of the sea.

Lilith Ritual Bath Scrub

This scrub is a powerful, all-natural body scrub designed to help you connect with your inner strength, confidence, and divine feminine energy. Infused with rose petals, which are associated with love and beauty, and patchouli, known for its grounding and sensual properties, this scrub is perfect for use in a self-care routine or as part of a spiritual bath ritual.

Ingredients:

1 cup sea salt
1/2 cup almond oil
1/4 cup dried rose petals, crushed
5 drops patchouli essential oil
5 drops rose essential oil
Instructions:

In a medium-sized mixing bowl, combine the sea salt and almond oil. Stir the ingredients together until they are well mixed and the salt is evenly coated in the oil.

Add the crushed rose petals to the salt and oil mixture, stirring them in until they are evenly distributed throughout the scrub.

Add the patchouli and rose essential oils to the mixture. Stir the ingredients together to ensure the essential oils are evenly distributed throughout the scrub.

Transfer the Lilith Empowerment Bath Scrub to a clean, airtight container, such as a glass jar with a tight-fitting lid. Store the scrub in a cool, dry place, away from direct sunlight.

To use the scrub, scoop a small amount of the mixture into your hands and gently massage it onto your wet skin in circular motions. Focus on areas where you'd like to cultivate self-love, empowerment, and divine feminine energy. Rinse the scrub off with warm water and pat your skin dry with a clean towel.

Enjoy the soft, smooth, and revitalized feeling of your skin after using the Lilith Empowerment Bath Scrub. Incorporate this scrub into your self-care routine or use it as part of a spiritual bath ritual to enhance your connection to the powerful energies of Lilith and the divine feminine.

Aphrodite's Goats Milk & Salt Beauty Scrub

Ingredients:

1/2 cup finely ground sea salt
1/2 cup Dead Sea salt

1/2 cup finely ground Epsom salt

1 cup pink Himalayan salt

1/2 cup powdered goat milk

1 tablespoon vitamin E oil

1 tablespoon aloe vera extract

10 drops rose essential oil

10 drops vanilla essential oil

1/4 cup dried red rose buds

1/4 cup dried jasmine flowers

1/4 cup dried heather flowers

Instructions:

In a mixing bowl, combine all the salts, powdered goat milk, and vitamin E oil.

Mix well, making sure the ingredients are evenly distributed.

Add the aloe vera extract, rose essential oil, and vanilla essential oil to the mixture.

Stir the ingredients again until everything is well combined.

Add the dried red rose buds, jasmine flowers, and heather flowers to the mixture and stir again.

Transfer the scrub to a jar with an airtight lid.

To use the scrub, simply wet your skin and apply a small amount of the mixture in a circular motion, paying special attention to rough areas. Rinse thoroughly with warm water.

This Aphrodite-inspired Beauty Goat Milk & Salt Scrub is perfect for enhancing your natural beauty and invoking the goddess of love and beauty herself. The mixture of salts and powdered goat milk gently exfoliates your skin, while the vitamin E oil and aloe vera extract nourish and moisturize it. The essential oils of rose and vanilla add a luxurious scent to the scrub, while the dried red rose buds, jasmine flowers, and heather flowers infuse it with the goddess's sacred energy. Enjoy the luxurious and sensual experience of this scrub, and let it help you connect with your own inner goddess.

Forging Your Own Path

As we reach the final section of this book on Green Witchcraft, it is important to remember that the journey of each practitioner is unique and deeply personal. Forging your own path is a crucial aspect of the practice, as it allows you to grow and evolve in a way that resonates with your individual beliefs, values, and goals. By embracing your authentic self and being open to exploration, you can create a spiritual practice that is meaningful and fulfilling.

One of the first steps to forging your own path is to reflect on your own experiences and beliefs. Take the time to consider what aspects of Green Witchcraft resonate with you the most and how they align with your personal values. This introspection will help you identify the core elements of your practice and provide a solid foundation for your spiritual journey.

Next, consider the sources of knowledge and inspiration that speak to you the most. While there is a wealth of information available on Green Witchcraft and related practices, it is essential to find the resources that resonate with you and your unique perspective. Be open to learning from a variety of sources, such as books, workshops, online forums, and experienced practitioners, but always trust your intuition and discernment when incorporating new ideas and techniques into your practice.

As you develop your own path, it's essential to cultivate a relationship with the natural world around you. Explore the local flora and fauna, observe the cycles of the Earth and the moon, and pay attention to the subtle shifts in energy that occur throughout the seasons. By deepening your connection to the environment, you will gain a greater understanding of the natural rhythms and energies that influence your practice.

Creating a personal ritual space is another essential aspect of forging your own path. Whether indoors or outdoors, this sacred space serves as a sanctuary for your practice and a reflection of your unique spiritual journey. Design your space to include elements that hold personal significance, such as representations of the elements, symbols of your chosen deities, or items from nature that resonate with you.

Incorporating personal rituals and practices that align with your beliefs and values is another vital part of forging your own path. Experiment with different techniques and methods, such as meditation, visualization, spell work, or divination, and pay attention to how they impact your personal energy and connection to the natural world. Over time, you will discover which practices resonate with you the most and help you deepen your connection to Green Witchcraft.

Finally, remember that the path of the Green Witch is one of continuous growth and transformation. As you evolve and learn, be open to adapting your practice and embracing new experiences. By staying true to yourself and remaining open to the wisdom of nature and the universe, you can create a fulfilling and empowering spiritual journey that is uniquely your own.

Further Reading

"The Green Witch: Your Complete Guide to the Natural Magic of Herbs, Flowers, Essential Oils, and More" by Arin Murphy-Hiscock

This comprehensive guide covers the foundations of Green Witchcraft, providing detailed information on working with herbs, flowers, essential oils, and other natural materials. A perfect resource for beginners and experienced practitioners alike.

"Earth Power: Techniques of Natural Magic" by Scott Cunningham

Scott Cunningham's classic work introduces readers to the power and energy of the Earth and its natural elements. This book covers a wide range of natural magic practices, including elemental work, crystal magic, and herb lore.

"Hedgewitch Book of Days: Spells, Rituals, and Recipes for the Magical Year" by Mandy Mitchell

This practical guide offers daily practices, spells, rituals, and recipes to align with the cycles of the year. A great resource for those seeking to incorporate Green Witchcraft into their daily lives.

"Garden Witchery: Magick from the Ground Up" by Ellen Dugan

Ellen Dugan shares her experience and knowledge of Green Witchcraft, focusing on the magic and energy found in the garden. This book offers tips on growing and harvesting magical herbs, creating sacred outdoor spaces, and working with the spirits of the land.

"The Witching Herbs: 13 Essential Plants and Herbs for Your Magical Garden" by Harold Roth

This book delves into the magical properties and uses of 13 essential plants and herbs for the Green Witch's garden. It provides practical advice on cultivation and care, as well as guidance on using these powerful plants in rituals and spell work.

"To Walk a Pagan Path: Practical Spirituality for Every Day" by Alaric Albertsson

Alaric Albertsson offers guidance on incorporating Pagan spirituality and Green Witchcraft practices into everyday life. With a focus on connecting with nature, the book provides rituals, meditations, and other practices designed to deepen the reader's connection to the Earth.

"Plant Spirit Witchcraft: Green Magick, Herbalism & Spirituality" by Christopher Penczak

In this exploration of plant spirit magic, Christopher Penczak delves into the spiritual aspects of Green Witchcraft and herbalism. Readers will learn how to connect with the spirits of plants and use their wisdom in rituals and magic.

"The Druid's Garden: A Guide to Growing and Using Magical Plants" by Phyllida Anam-Aire

Phyllida Anam-Aire offers practical advice on growing and using magical plants, with a focus on the wisdom and traditions of the Druids. The book includes detailed profiles of various plants, along with guidance on how to use them in rituals, spells, and other magical practices.

"Braiding Sweetgrass: Indigenous Wisdom, Scientific Knowledge, and the Teachings of Plants" by Robin Wall Kimmerer

This beautifully written book combines indigenous wisdom and scientific knowledge to explore the interconnectedness of humans and the natural world. A must-read for those interested in deepening their understanding of the spiritual aspects of Green Witchcraft and our relationship with the Earth.

"The Earthwise Herbal: A Complete Guide to Old World Medicinal Plants" by Matthew Wood

This comprehensive guide to Old World medicinal plants offers detailed profiles of various herbs, including their historical uses, magical properties, and practical applications. A valuable resource for Green Witches seeking to expand their knowledge of herbalism and plant magic.

Correspondences

In the practice of witchcraft, correspondences are the associations or connections made between various elements, objects, colors, or symbols and their specific energies, qualities, or intentions. These associations can help witches and practitioners of magic to focus their intentions and enhance their rituals or spells. For example, certain herbs, crystals, or colors might be associated with healing, love, or protection. By understanding these correspondences, a witch can select the appropriate tools and ingredients for their magical workings, ensuring that the energies they draw upon align with their desired outcomes. Correspondences can be found in various magical traditions and belief systems, and they often reflect the unique cultural, historical, or geographical contexts from which they arise. It's important to remember that while many correspondences are widely agreed upon, personal experiences and beliefs can also influence the associations one makes, allowing for a deeply individual and meaningful practice.

The following is a list of commonly associated properties of different things you might utilize in your practice, these description are brief for reference purposes, for more detailed information check the corresponding section of the book.

Crystals and Stones

Amethyst: Enhances intuition and spiritual growth; promotes calmness and balance.

Aquamarine: Encourages clarity, courage, and communication; eases stress and anxiety.

Black Tourmaline: Offers powerful protection against negative energy; grounds and stabilizes.

Bloodstone: Boosts strength, courage, and vitality; enhances decision-making and intuition.

Carnelian: Stimulates creativity, motivation, and personal power; supports reproductive health.

Citrine: Attracts abundance and success; promotes self-confidence and positivity.

Clear Quartz: Amplifies energy and intention; enhances psychic abilities and spiritual growth.

Emerald: Promotes love, loyalty, and emotional healing; enhances memory and wisdom.

Fluorite: Increases focus, clarity, and organization; balances mental and emotional energies.

Garnet: Enhances passion, sensuality, and self-confidence; supports grounding and courage.

Hematite: Grounds and protects; boosts self-esteem, willpower, and confidence.

Jade: Attracts good luck, prosperity, and love; encourages emotional balance and harmony.

Labradorite: Enhances intuition, psychic abilities, and spiritual insight; protects the aura.

Lapis Lazuli: Stimulates wisdom, truth, and self-awareness; enhances intellectual abilities.

Malachite: Encourages transformation, growth, and emotional healing; protects against negativity.

Moonstone: Enhances intuition, psychic abilities, and spiritual insight; supports fertility and emotional balance.

Obsidian: Offers strong protection and grounding; supports emotional healing and shadow work.

Peridot: Attracts abundance, prosperity, and happiness; encourages growth and renewal.

Rhodonite: Promotes emotional healing, self-love, and forgiveness; reduces anxiety and stress.

Rose Quartz: Attracts love and compassion; supports emotional healing and self-love.

Selenite: Cleanses and charges other crystals; connects to divine light and spiritual guidance.

Smoky Quartz: Grounds and protects; promotes emotional healing and stress relief.

Sodalite: Enhances intuition, communication, and self-expression; promotes emotional balance.

Sunstone: Boosts self-confidence, motivation, and personal power; attracts abundance and joy.

Tiger's Eye: Encourages courage, focus, and personal power; supports grounding and protection.

Tourmalinated Quartz: Combines the properties of Clear Quartz and Black Tourmaline for amplified protection and grounding.

Turquoise: Promotes communication, self-expression, and emotional healing; attracts abundance and success.

Unakite: Supports emotional healing, balance, and spiritual growth; promotes self-love and compassion.

White Agate: Encourages emotional balance, protection, and grounding; supports mental clarity and focus.

Yellow Jasper: Boosts self-confidence, motivation, and personal power; supports grounding and protection.

Candles

Black: Absorbs and removes negativity; promotes grounding, protection, and banishing.

Brown: Represents grounding, stability, and balance; attracts home and family matters, as well as animal healing.

Dark Blue: Represents wisdom, truth, and spiritual insight; promotes psychic abilities and intuition.

Gold: Represents the Sun's energy and masculine power; attracts success, abundance, and personal power.

Gray: Neutralizes negative energy and promotes balance; supports decision-making and finding middle ground.

Green: Attracts abundance, prosperity, and growth; promotes healing and fertility.

Light Blue: Encourages peace, tranquility, and emotional healing; enhances communication and self-expression.

Orange: Stimulates creativity, success, and enthusiasm; attracts opportunities and positive change.

Pink: Attracts love, friendship, and romance; encourages emotional healing and self-love.

Purple: Enhances spiritual growth, psychic abilities, and wisdom; supports meditation and divine connection.

Red: Symbolizes passion, love, and courage; enhances vitality, energy, and motivation.

Silver: Represents the Moon's energy and feminine power; enhances psychic abilities and intuition.

White: Represents purity, cleansing, and protection; can substitute for any other candle color.

Yellow: Represents happiness, intellect, and communication; boosts self-confidence and personal power.

Incense

Amber: Attracts love, healing, and protection; supports emotional balance and spiritual growth.

Cedar: Represents strength, protection, and grounding; attracts positive energy and spiritual insight.

Cinnamon: Boosts energy, motivation, and success; supports protection and love.

Copal: Supports purification, protection, and spiritual growth; aids in meditation and divine connection.

Dragon's Blood: Enhances protection, strength, and courage; supports banishing negativity and attracting love.

Eucalyptus: Promotes healing, protection, and clarity; supports respiratory health and emotional balance.

Frankincense: Promotes spiritual growth, protection, and purification; enhances meditation and divine connection.

Jasmine: Enhances love, sensuality, and spiritual insight; supports emotional healing and self-confidence.

Lavender: Promotes tranquility, harmony, and emotional healing; supports restful sleep and stress relief.

Lemongrass: Supports mental clarity, emotional balance, and spiritual growth; attracts positive energy and repels negativity.

Myrrh: Supports spiritual awakening, protection, and healing; aids in meditation and balancing energies.

Nag Champa: Encourages relaxation, meditation, and spiritual awareness; supports inner peace and tranquility.

Palo Santo: Cleanses and purifies negative energy; promotes grounding, healing, and spiritual growth.

Patchouli: Attracts love, prosperity, and abundance; supports grounding and balance.

Pine: Represents grounding, strength, and cleansing; supports protection and attracting prosperity.

Rose: Symbolizes love, happiness, and emotional healing; attracts love and enhances relationships.

Sage: Purifies and cleanses negative energy; promotes healing, wisdom, and spiritual growth.

Sandalwood: Encourages relaxation, peace, and spiritual awareness; aids in meditation and attracts positive energy.

Vanilla: Encourages happiness, love, and sensuality; supports mental clarity and emotional healing.

Ylang Ylang: Enhances love, sensuality, and emotional healing; promotes self-confidence and spiritual growth.

Herbs and Teas

Basil: Attracts wealth, love, and protection; dispels negativity.

Black Tea: Boosts strength, protection, and grounding; commonly used for shielding

Calendula: Promotes healing, protection, and psychic development.

Chamomile: Encourages relaxation, healing, and attracts abundance.

Dandelion: Enhances divination, wishes, and spiritual growth.

Elderflower: Offers protection, healing, and aids in banishing negativity.

Frankincense: Boosts spirituality, meditation, and protection.

Ginger: Enhances love, success, and personal power.

Hibiscus: Stimulates love, passion, and psychic abilities.

Jasmine: Attracts love, prosperity, and enhances psychic dreams.

Lavender: Brings peace, love, and harmony; encourages restful sleep.

Lemon Balm: Attracts love, success, and promotes emotional healing.

Mugwort: Enhances psychic abilities, dream work, and astral travel.

Nettle: Offers protection, healing, and helps to dispel negativity.

Peppermint: Boosts mental clarity, healing, and attracts prosperity.

Rose: Symbolizes love, beauty, and emotional healing.

Rosemary: Provides protection, love, and mental clarity; dispels negativity.

Sage: Purifies, protects, and promotes wisdom and spiritual growth.

Thyme: Enhances courage, healing, and draws in love.

Valerian: Encourages restful sleep, protection, and love.

Yarrow: Stimulates love, healing, and enhances courage and protection.

Fruit

Apple: Encourages love, wisdom, and healing.

Apricot: Attracts love, happiness, and emotional balance.

Avocado: Enhances beauty, love, and fertility.

Banana: Promotes abundance, prosperity, and sexuality.

Blackberry: Offers protection, healing, and attracts wealth.

Blueberry: Enhances protection, communication, and psychic abilities.

Cherry: Stimulates love, passion, and new beginnings.

Coconut: Enhances purification, protection, and chastity.

Fig: Encourages fertility, love, and spiritual insight.

Grape: Enhances abundance, prosperity, and fertility.

Lemon: Boosts cleansing, purification, and friendship.

Mango: Encourages love, sensuality, and spiritual growth.

Orange: Attracts love, joy, and overall well-being.

Papaya: Enhances love, protection, and spiritual healing.

Peach: Promotes love, fertility, and longevity.

Pear: Stimulates love, lust, and partnership.

Peppers: Stimulates passion, courage, and personal power

Pineapple: Attracts luck, prosperity, and hospitality.

Pumpkin: Enhances prosperity, protection, and spiritual growth.

Raspberry: Promotes protection, love, and healing relationships.

Strawberry: Encourages love, passion, and self-esteem.

Tomatoes: Encourages love, health, and protection from negativity

Watermelon: Enhances fertility, sexuality, and emotional healing.

Vegetables

Artichoke: Encourages growth, protection, and healing.

Asparagus: Enhances fertility, spiritual awakening, and strengthens psychic abilities.

Beetroot: Stimulates love, passion, and grounding.

Broccoli: Promotes abundance, protection, and strength.

Cabbage: Encourages luck, prosperity, and protection.

Carrot: Enhances fertility, vision, and grounding.

Cauliflower: Stimulates spiritual growth, purification, and inner wisdom.

Celery: Promotes psychic powers, mental clarity, and concentration.

Corn: Represents abundance, fertility, and the harvest.

Cucumber: Encourages healing, fertility, and emotional balance.

Eggplant: Enhances protection, abundance, and transformation.

Garlic: Provides protection, healing, and purification.

Kale: Encourages strength, protection, and abundance.

Lettuce: Promotes peace, tranquility, and restful sleep.

Onion: Enhances protection, purification, and banishing negativity.

Peas: Stimulates love, friendship, and abundance.

Potato: Encourages grounding, sustenance, and protection.

Pumpkin: Enhances prosperity, protection, and spiritual growth.

Radish: Provides protection, purification, and banishing negativity.

Spinach: Promotes strength, abundance, and spiritual growth.

Altar Covers/Ritual Cloths

Black: Represents grounding, protection, and banishing negative energies; commonly used for transformation and shadow work

Blue: Symbolizes communication, truth, and peace; often used for healing, meditation, and spiritual growth rituals

Brown: Represents grounding, stability, and earth energy; commonly used for grounding, protection, and home blessing rituals

Gold: Represents solar energy, success, and prosperity; commonly used for abundance, success, and manifestation rituals

Green: Represents abundance, growth, and prosperity; commonly used for money spells, fertility, and earth-based rituals

Orange: Symbolizes energy, vitality, and courage; often used for creativity, confidence, and attraction rituals

Purple: Represents spiritual power, psychic abilities, and wisdom; commonly used for enhancing intuition, spiritual growth, and divination

Pink: Symbolizes love, harmony, and compassion; often used for self-love, relationship healing, and friendship rituals

Red: Symbolizes passion, love, and courage; often used for love spells, empowerment, and strength rituals

Silver: Symbolizes lunar energy, intuition, and psychic abilities; often used for moon rituals, psychic development, and goddess work

White: Symbolizes purity, spirituality, and divine connection; often used for healing, protection, and peace rituals

Yellow: Represents intellect, creativity, and happiness; commonly used for inspiration, learning, and success spells

Wood

Apple: Symbolizes love, healing, and abundance; often used for love spells, fertility, and working with goddess energies.

Ash: Represents transformation, healing, and balance; commonly used for spiritual growth, protection, and invoking divine energies.

Birch: Symbolizes renewal, protection, and purification; often used for cleansing, new beginnings, and invoking protective energies.

Cedar: Represents purification, balance, and healing; commonly used for cleansing spaces, protection, and spiritual growth.

Cherry: Symbolizes love, passion, and self-expression; often used for enhancing romantic energies, creative inspiration, and emotional healing.

Elder: Symbolizes wisdom, protection, and transformation; often used for banishing negativity, working with ancestral energies, and connecting with the spirit realm.

Fig: Represents fertility, abundance, and spiritual insight; commonly used for enhancing spiritual growth, connecting with divine wisdom, and manifesting desires.

Hawthorn: Symbolizes purification, protection, and spiritual growth; often used for warding off negative energies, enhancing psychic abilities, and connecting with the fae.

Lemon: Represents purification, clarity, and revitalization; commonly used for cleansing energies, dispelling negativity, and revitalizing the spirit.

Maple: Represents love, balance, and abundance; commonly used for love spells, harmony, and manifestation.

Oak: Symbolizes strength, stability, and wisdom; often used for protection, grounding, and connecting with ancestral energies.

Olive: Symbolizes peace, wisdom, and healing; often used for promoting harmony, accessing inner wisdom, and encouraging physical and emotional healing.

Orange: Symbolizes abundance, success, and creativity; often used for attracting prosperity, boosting confidence, and inspiring creative pursuits.

Peach: Represents abundance, joy, and fertility; commonly used for attracting happiness, love, and prosperity in personal and professional life.

Pine: Symbolizes resilience, abundance, and longevity; often used for prosperity, grounding, and connecting with nature spirits.

Plum: Symbolizes transformation, inner strength, and intuition; often used for spiritual growth, psychic development, and overcoming obstacles.

Rowan: Represents protection, inspiration, and psychic abilities; commonly used for warding off negative energies, enhancing intuition, and invoking inspiration.

Willow: Represents intuition, healing, and emotional balance; commonly used for moon rituals, divination, and enhancing psychic abilities.

Yew: Represents transformation, rebirth, and longevity; commonly used for ancestor work, spirit communication, and life transitions.

Moon Phases

New Moon: New beginnings, initiation, and manifesting; ideal for setting intentions, starting new projects, and planting seeds for growth.

Waxing Crescent: Growth, expansion, and increasing positivity; suitable for attracting abundance, increasing motivation, and strengthening intentions set during the New Moon.

First Quarter: Determination, decision-making, and action; perfect for pushing through obstacles, making important decisions, and focusing on personal goals.

Waxing Gibbous: Refinement, adjustment, and fine-tuning; great for analyzing progress, refining goals, and making necessary adjustments to stay on track.

Full Moon: Completion, celebration, and gratitude; an ideal time for releasing what no longer serves you, celebrating achievements, and expressing gratitude for blessings received.

Waning Gibbous: Reflection, introspection, and sharing wisdom; suitable for self-assessment, contemplation, and sharing knowledge with others.

Last Quarter: Release, letting go, and forgiveness; perfect for releasing negativity, breaking bad habits, and practicing forgiveness towards oneself and others.

Waning Crescent: Surrender, rest, and recuperation; ideal for embracing restorative practices, finding closure, and preparing for the next cycle with the upcoming New Moon.

Heavenly Bodies

Sun: Vitality, success, confidence, and leadership; associated with personal power, creativity, and the life force energy.

Moon: Intuition, emotions, psychic abilities, and the subconscious mind; connected to nurturing, receptivity, and the ebb and flow of life.

Mercury: Communication, intellect, learning, and travel; linked to thought processes, decision-making, and adaptability.

Venus: Love, beauty, harmony, and relationships; associated with attraction, aesthetics, self-worth, and balance in partnerships.

Mars: Courage, passion, drive, and assertiveness; connected to motivation, ambition, and taking action.

Jupiter: Expansion, growth, abundance, and wisdom; associated with optimism, prosperity, and higher learning.

Saturn: Discipline, structure, responsibility, and karmic lessons; linked to boundaries, limitations, and long-term planning.

Uranus: Change, innovation, rebellion, and awakening; connected to sudden transformations, breakthroughs, and freedom from restrictions.

Neptune: Dreams, spirituality, intuition, and mysticism; associated with imagination, psychic abilities, and the dissolution of boundaries.

Pluto: Transformation, regeneration, power, and rebirth; linked to deep healing, release of old patterns, and spiritual growth.

Futhark Runes

Fehu: Wealth, abundance, prosperity, and growth.

Uruz: Strength, vitality, courage, and healing.

Thurisaz: Protection, defense, and overcoming obstacles.

Ansuz: Communication, wisdom, and divine guidance.

Raidho: Travel, movement, and taking action.

Kenaz: Creativity, inspiration, and knowledge.

Gebo: Gifts, balance, and partnerships.

Wunjo: Joy, harmony, and success.

Hagalaz: Transformation, change, and disruption.

Nauthiz: Need, resourcefulness, and endurance.

Isa: Stillness, patience, and reflection.

Jera: Cycles, harvest, and natural patterns.

Eihwaz: Stability, protection, and spiritual growth.

Perthro: Mystery, fate, and hidden knowledge.

Algiz: Protection, guidance, and connecting with higher powers.

Sowilo: Success, energy, and the power of the sun.

Tiwaz: Honor, justice, and leadership.

Berkano: Fertility, growth, and new beginnings.

Ehwaz: Harmony, partnership, and cooperation.

Mannaz: Humanity, relationships, and self-awareness.

Laguz: Emotions, intuition, and the power of water.

Ingwaz: Fertility, growth, and inner potential.

Dagaz: Enlightenment, breakthroughs, and transformation.

Othala: Ancestry, heritage, and spiritual inheritance.

Terms and Definitions

The following is a list of terms that might be useful to learn while continuing your journey, some of them I've already mentioned and some I haven't and am including here since I didn't include elsewhere for one reason or another.

Altar – an elevated surface used to perform rituals and make offerings.

Amulet – an object or charm worn to protect or bring luck.

Athame – a ritual knife used to symbolically draw energy or to direct energy.

Ancestors – those who have passed on, whom many pagans honor and call upon for guidance.

Augury – divination by observing the behavior of birds.

Astrology – the practice of interpreting celestial events to gain insight into the future.

Aspergillum – a tool used to sprinkle water, wine, or other liquids during ritual.

Astral Plane – a non-physical realm believed to exist beyond the physical world.

Arcana – cards used as part of a divination system.

Blessing - A ritual or prayer that bestows good wishes, health, and fortune.

Banishing - A ritual used to dispel or remove negative energy or entities.

Banishment - A magical act in which a person or being is banished from a particular space or area.

Besom - A broom used in Wiccan rituals for blessing, purifying, and warding.

Book of Shadows - A journal or book used to record spells, rituals, and other magical information.

Brew - A potion or mixture of herbs, oils, and other ingredients used to create a magical effect.

Cauldron - A large metal pot used in rituals and spellwork.

Charms - Items used in rituals, like amulets and talismans, to create a magical effect.

Coven - A group of witches that typically meets regularly for rituals and spellwork.

Conjuration - A ritual conducted to summon a spirit or supernatural being.

Craft - Another name for witchcraft.

Crystals - Stones used in rituals and spellwork to boost energy and provide protection.

Curses - Spells intended to produce a negative effect.

Candles - Used to signify different intentions and energies in rituals and spell work.

Circles - A boundary drawn in the form of a circle that is used to form a sacred space for rituals.

Divination - Divination is the practice of using rituals, objects, symbols, and natural phenomena to gain insight into the past, present, and future.

Demonology - Demonology is the study of demons, their origins and activities. It is used as a tool to identify and understand the spiritual forces in our lives and how they can be used for good or ill.

Druids - Druids are a group of ancient Celtic priests who practiced religious rituals, healing, and divination. They were believed to have deep spiritual knowledge and were often consulted as wise men or counselors.

Deity - Deity is a being or force of great power that is worshipped by humans as a supernatural being.

Deity Invocation - Deity invocation is a ritual used to call upon a particular deity and ask for their assistance. It typically involves invoking the deity's name and then offering prayers of gratitude and supplication.

Divination Tools - Divination tools are objects used to help interpret the unknown. Common divination tools include tarot cards, runes, pendulums, and scrying mirrors.

Devotional Prayer - Devotional prayer is a type of prayer used to express reverence and adoration to a particular deity. It typically involves repeating mantras or sacred phrases, as well as meditating on the deity's presence.

Elemental Magic - Magic that works with the four elements - earth, air, fire, and water - to create powerful rituals and spells.

Energy Work - A form of magic that uses energy and intention to manifest desires.

Enchantment - A type of spell or ritual that is used to enchant or influence an object or person.

Evocation - A type of ritual or spell that is used to summon or call upon spirits or energies.

Extispicy - The practice of divination by interpreting the entrails of animals, usually done by a shaman or practitioner.

Elemental Invocations - Invocations used to call upon particular elements - earth, air, fire, and water - to aid in rituals and spells.

Enchantments - Spells used to protect, bless, or bring luck to a person, place, or thing

Familiar - A creature that is connected to a witch, often in the form of an animal.

Faery - A spirit, usually of the Celtic tradition.

Familiar Spirit - A spirit that is connected to a witch, often in the form of an animal.

Famulus - A servant or assistant to a witch.

Farseeing - The ability to see events in the future.

Fey - A type of magical creature.

Fylgja - In Norse mythology, a spirit that accompanies a person, often taking the form of an animal.

Galdr - An Old Norse term that refers to singing or chanting. It's still used today in some pagan rituals.

Glamour - A term that refers to an enchantment that alters the perception of the viewer.

Grimoire - A book of rituals, spells, and knowledge related to magic and/or religion.

Grounding - A ritual to connect with the energies of the Earth and to clear the mind.

Hallows - The eight Sabbats of the Pagan Wheel of the Year.

Handfasting - A Celtic ritual signifying betrothal and marriage.

Hex - A spell or enchantment used to cause harm.

Herbology - The practice of using herbs and plants as medicines.

Horned God - A masculine deity in Paganism representing the cycle of death and rebirth, the Hunter, and the Lord of the

Wild.

Horoscope - A chart of the positions of the planets and signs of the zodiac at a specific time.

Incantation - A spoken spell or ritual that is used to invoke or evoke supernatural powers or forces.

Invocation - The practice of calling upon or summoning divine or supernatural beings, spirits, or forces.

Invoke - To call upon or summon a supernatural being, spirit, or force.

Initiation - A ritual that marks the transition of an individual into a particular role or group.

Jinx - A curse or hex designed to bring bad luck or misfortune to a person or place.

Joss Stick - A thin stick of incense used in Chinese ancestor worship and for spiritual purification.

Justiciar - A practitioner of justice and law within the spiritual community.

Ka - A Ka is an individual's spiritual double and the life force that sustains their life.

Kavach - Kavach is a Sanskrit term for a magical amulet or charm.

Kefa - Kefa is a type of Jewish prayer consisting of the recital of a set of words or sentences.

King's Evil - King's Evil is an old belief that a king's touch could cure a person of a range of illnesses.

Kuei - Kuei is an ancient Chinese term for ghosts, evil spirits, and other supernatural entities.

Lunar - Relating to or governed by the cycles of the moon.

Litha - A sabbat or celebration falling on June 21st, marking the summer solstice.

Lore - The body of knowledge, traditions and cultural practices pertaining to a particular subject.

Leechcraft - Another term for folk healing and herbalism.

Lithomancy - A form of divination using crystals and gemstones.

Mabon - a pagan holiday celebrated around the Autumnal Equinox.

Magic - the practice of manipulating energy to bring about desired changes in the physical world.

Maleficarum - a term used to refer to negative spells or curses.

Mojo – an amulet or charm believed to have magical powers.

Moonstone – a type of gemstone associated with the moon and femininity.

Morrigan – a goddess of Irish mythology associated with battle and destiny.

Mysticism – the practice of seeking spiritual knowledge through contemplation, prayer, and intense study.

Necromancy - The practice of summoning the dead for divination or communication.

Nekyia - The ancient Greek ritual of connecting with the spirits of the underworld.

Nature Magic - A spiritual practice which uses natural elements and energies to create positive change.

Nyctophilia - The love of darkness, which is often associated with witchcraft and ritual work.

Paganism - The religious practices and beliefs of an ancient, pre-Christian religion found in many cultures throughout the world.

Pantheon - A group of gods or deities worshipped by a particular culture or religion.

Patron Deity - A specific god or goddess who is the special protector of a person, place, or thing.

Potentization - A ritual process used to increase the magical properties of an object or charm.

Protection Spell - A spell or ritual designed to keep away negative energy or to protect a person or place from harm.

Pyromancy - Divination using fire, such as reading the patterns of the flames or smoke from a burning fire.

Quabbalah - A system of mysticism and magick that originated in Jewish mysticism, it teaches the secrets of the universe and how to manipulate it.

Quarter - A period of three months, often divided into four quarters, used in pagan and wiccan rituals for marking the passing of the year.

Questing - A type of spiritual practice in which one seeks out knowledge and wisdom, often aided by a deity or spirit guide.

Quintessence - The fifth element, often seen as the spiritual component of all matter.

Quintet - A group of five practitioners who work together in pagan and wiccan rituals.

Quicken - To activate or "awaken" a spell or ritual.

Reiki - An alternative healing practice involving the use of universal energy.

Ritual - A ceremony or set of practices carried out to achieve a desired goal.

Rune Casting - A method of divination involving the use of runes.

Ritual Circle - A circle used for the purpose of performing

rituals in Wicca.

Rede of the Wiccae - A set of guidelines for the ethical practice of Wicca.

Samhain - A Wiccan holiday celebrated on November 1st, marking the end of the harvest season and the beginning of winter.

Solitary Practice - This term is used to refer to the practice of witchcraft, paganism and ritual work without the involvement of covens or other groups.

Sabbat - Sabbats are the eight major festivals that are celebrated throughout the year and are fundamental to the practice of witchcraft.

Shamanism - Shamanism is a practice of spiritual healing, divination and communication with the spirit world.

Spellcasting - Spellcasting refers to the practice of creating and invoking spells and rituals to achieve a desired effect.

Sigil - Sigils are symbols that are used to represent an individual's intent and focus energy towards a desired outcome.

Shadow Work - Shadow work is the process of confronting and healing the parts of one's psyche that are hidden from conscious view.

Sacred Space - Sacred Space is an area that is consecrated and purified for the purpose of performing rituals and spellwork.

Scrying - Scrying is a form of divination that involves gazing into a reflective surface or object in order to gain insight and seek answers.

Spell Jar - Spell jars are containers that are filled with herbs, crystals, and other magical items to help focus and store energy for a specific spell or ritual.

Talisman - An object believed to be endowed with magical powers to protect or bring good luck.

Tarot Cards - A set of cards used for divination or fortune-telling.

Theurgy - The practice of performing rituals to invoke or placate supernatural beings.

Totem - A spirit being, sacred object, or symbol that serves as an emblem of a group of people, such as a family, clan, lineage, or tribe.

Trance - A state of consciousness in which a person is in between wakefulness and sleep.

Transmutation - The process of changing the form, nature, or substance of something.

Thaumaturgy - The practice of performing acts of magic or sorcery.

In Conclusion

As you conclude this journey through the realm of witchcraft and the path of the green witch, remember that the information within these pages is just the beginning of your exploration. The natural world is vast, rich, and ever-changing, offering countless opportunities for growth and connection. Embrace the beauty and magic that surrounds you, allowing it to guide you on a path towards spiritual actualization and a deeper understanding of the interconnectedness of all living things.

Thank you for taking the first step on this transformative journey with me. May your heart be filled with the love and warmth of the earth, and may your spirit be uplifted by the boundless energy of the elements. Continue to nurture your connection to nature, learning from its cycles and wisdom, and embody the essence of the green witch in all aspects of your life. Let this book serve as a starting point, a foundation upon which you can build and grow, as you continue to explore the vast and mystical world of green witchcraft. Blessed be!

-Brittany

Disclaimer: Always take safety precautions when doing any ritual. Be careful if using stoves or any heat sources and always make sure to have proper ventilation. This information is educational and religious, it is not to be taken as professional medical advice, always consult with a medical professional first and foremost. Use this book at your own peril: I'm not responsible for any unintended consequences. Never ingest anything unless you're completely sure it's safe and you aren't allergic. Always be wary of the potential risk of forcing your will onto others, as there can be unintended consequences. Do not commit any crimes, such as trespassing, when conducting your rituals: I don't have a spell to get you out of jail!

Much love,
Brittany

If you've enjoyed the book, please consider giving me a review on Amazon and following me on Instagram and Facebook:
facebook.com/xobrittanynightshade
@Nightshade_Apothecary

Merry met!
And merry part!
-Brittany Nightshade

Printed in Great Britain
by Amazon